Building a Panel Bedroom Suite

Joseph D. Grove

Schiffer Publishing Ltd
4880 Lower Valley Road • Atglen, PA 19310

Other Schiffer Books on Related Subjects:
Creating a Fine Art Entry Table. Robert Ortiz. ISBN: 978-0-7643-3071-1. $24.99
Mind & Hand: Contemporary Studio Furniture. The Furniture Society. ISBN: 978-0-7643-4115-1. $29.99

Library of Congress Control Number: 2012955353

Cover and book design by John P. Cheek
Type set in Zurich BT/Zurich BT

ISBN: 978-0-7643-4159-5
Printed in China

Schiffer Books are available at special discounts for bulk purchases for sales promotions or premiums. Special editions, including personalized covers, corporate imprints, and excerpts can be created in large quantities for special needs. For more information contact the publisher:

Published by Schiffer Publishing, Ltd.
4880 Lower Valley Road
Atglen, PA 19310
Phone: (610) 593-1777; Fax: (610) 593-2002
E-mail: Info@schifferbooks.com

For the largest selection of fine reference books on this and related subjects, please visit our website at
www.schifferbooks.com
We are always looking for people to write books on new and related subjects. If you have an idea for a book, please contact us at
proposals@schifferbooks.com

This book may be purchased from the publisher.
Please try your bookstore first.
You may write for a free catalog.

In Europe, Schiffer books are distributed by
Bushwood Books
6 Marksbury Ave.
Kew Gardens
Surrey TW9 4JF England
Phone: 44 (0) 20 8392 8585; Fax: 44 (0) 20 8392 9876
E-mail: info@bushwoodbooks.co.uk
Website: www.bushwoodbooks.co.uk

Dedication

This book is dedicated to my wife, Katina, and children, Benjamin and Julianne. They have provided great encouragement throughout the years. Although I have held several jobs, woodworking is my passion. My wife recognizes this and supports my decisions. To my parents, Chester and Dorothy: Thank you for teaching me the value of hard work and honesty. To my in-laws, Bill and Vonnie: Thank you for getting me started down this path and allowing me to use your tools while I saved change to buy my own.

Acknowledgments

Thanks to my customers who have asked for everything that is not available in a store. These requests have allowed me to experience the process of furniture making from drawing a sketch to building the final product.

Thank you, Mrs. Wanda Grove (no known relation) for commissioning the furniture in this book. They were unique in their design and worthy of sharing their understated elegance with other furniture makers.

Thank you, Dr. and Mrs. Pellow for advice to get this book started and encouragement as I built furniture for their home.

To the staff of Schiffer Publishing, thank you for your understanding and the opportunity to share my skills. Juggling a full time job, a growing furniture business, family life, and writing a book is quite a handful.

Contents

Often a log has inner stress that is relieved when cut into planks. Most pieces are straight and of the same thickness throughout its length at the time of sawing. Drying brings each piece to its resting form. Whether a bow, twist, or cup exists in a piece of lumber, ways to fix these issues are straightforward.

Issue: *Bow*

Bowing lumber can most easily be dealt with by cutting the plank into shorter sections, which shortens the height of the arc.

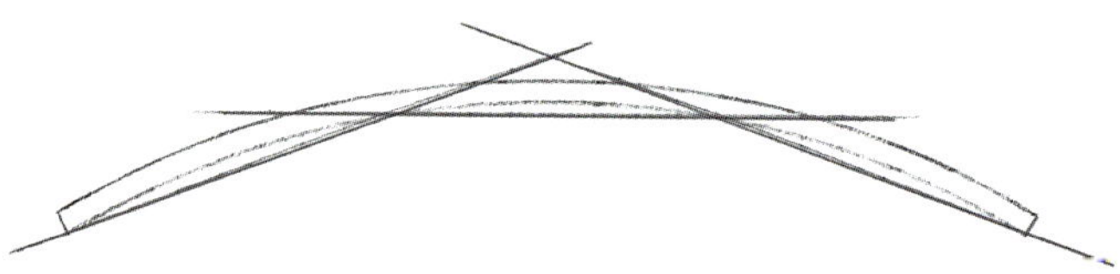

Remedy:

After cutting into sections, run each piece over a jointer with the bow up so the ends are planed flat, removing only 1/64″ of an inch per pass. When the arched side is flat, go to the surface planer. Set the planer height slightly lower than the thickest part on the plank. Pass through the surface planer in successive passes until the whole piece is of uniform thickness.

Issue: *Twist*

Twisted boards can cause problems especially when gluing together individual boards to make panels. Wide boards can be placed on a flat surface such as the table saw to determine the twist and its severity.

Remedy:

The section of the board that touches the flat surface is what needs to be removed to flatten one face. A scribble of chalk will show your progress. First run the end of the board that is touching the table over the jointer taking off only 1/64″ of an inch until approximately the mid-point of the board. Turn the board end for end and run the end that is touching over the jointer. Sit the piece back on the flat surface to check your progress. Continue this process until one side is free from rocking. Now run the board through the surface planer with its height set for the thickest part of the board. When the top is completely flat, run the side that was previously flattened by the jointer through your planer. This will create a board of uniform thickness that is also flat.

Issue: *Cupping*

Cupping happens as a board is trying to straighten its growth rings. This can be noticed by looking at the end grain of the board.

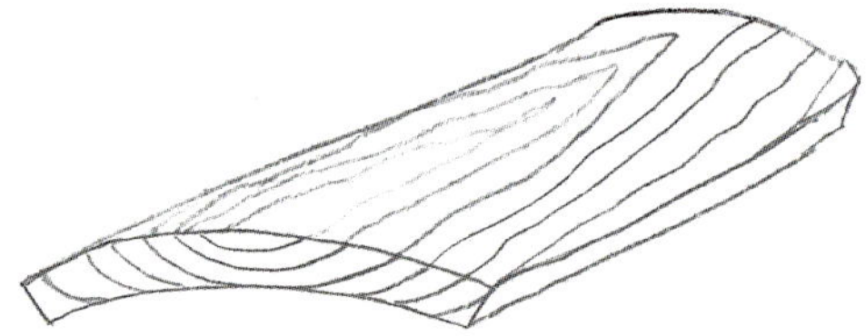

Remedies:

Running a cupped board through a thickness planer with the arched part up is the first step to flattening the board. When enough area has been planed to create a flat surface, turn the board over and run the second side through the planer. Taking equal amounts off each side will help keep the board from cupping more to relieve additional stress. *OR*…

Saw the board lengthwise (rip cut), lessening the height of the arc, then plane with a thickness planer.

Gluing up Panels

Using boards 4-6 inches wide will aid in the flattening process and allow for arranging the boards as described further in the process.

Begin by cutting the pieces to be glued together 2″ longer than their finished length. Flatten each board to remove any twist, cup, or bow as outlined in the Methods of Work. Plane all boards to the required thickness plus 1/16″. Place the board on a flat surface while settling it on its edge. The first edge to be straightened should be the edge where only the ends are touching the flat surface. With the jointer fence set at 90 degrees to the table, run this edge through the jointer, removing 1/32″ per pass until the edge is straight. At the table saw, place the jointed edge against the fence and rip the board to create a parallel edge to the jointed edge. Smooth the edge just cut on the table saw by running it over the jointer. The board is now flat, straight, and ready to be a part of the assembled panel.

Achieving glued up panels that stay flat after the clamps are removed can be easily accomplished. By looking at the growth rings at the end of each board, alternate what I call "smiles and frowns."

Arrange the boards until the face of the panel appears almost seamless while maintaining the smiles and frowns. Mark an arrow with chalk on the boards to show their placement. Lay out the boards in their sequence on the clamps. Lay the first board flat and the others on their edge. Notice the chalk marks keep the pieces in their proper orientation. Apply an even layer of wood glue to the edges that are up. Lay all the pieces down and place spring clamps on the ends at each joint. Tighten the bar clamps while making sure the joints are close to flush across the panel. Check the underside of the panel for gaps away from the bar of the clamp. If there is a gap at the middle, decrease the clamp pressure. Gaps away from the bar at the ends of the clamps can be tapped down with a rubber mallet. The spring clamps can now be removed and the glue that squeezed out can be wiped off with a damp rag. By wiping off the excess glue, the panel is easier to sand and eliminates tear out if scraped later. After drying for a few hours, remove the bar clamps and remove any glue not removed initially. Panels can be sanded flat after allowing the glue to cure for 3-5 days. Since wood glue is water based, sanding the panel flat too early could possibly reveal raised joints later.

Begin by cutting the pieces to the dimensions on the cutting list. Marking each piece with chalk helps to clearly identify its location and the side that will be seen. This will be helpful in placement of dados and holes to be drilled as the building process continues.

Note: Glue up panels if your lumber isn't wide enough for the head and foot board panels. Set aside after clamping so they can dry while the joinery is being made.

Building the English Style Bed

Introduction

This bed was designed to complement an antique lingerie chest inherited by my client. Although unsure of the chest's age, the piece had its roots in England. It had been in their family for quite a few years. Taking design cues from the chest led to my design of the bed's legs and trim elements. Mahogany was my wood of choice to match the antique lingerie chest. This piece would appear equally impressive in cherry, walnut, or even painted maple.

English Bed Cut List (listed in inches)		
Qty	Dimensions	Description
2	2 ¼ x 2 ¼ x 21 ¼	Legs
2	3/4 x 3 x 55⅛	Rails
2	3/4 x 3 ¼ x 10 (1/2 TBE*)	Outer Stiles
2	3/4 x 2 ½ x 10 (1/2 TBE*)	Inner Stiles
3	1/4 x 9 ⅞ x 15 ½	Panels
1	3/4 x 3 x 59 ⅝	Top
1	3/4 x 1 x 53 ⅝	Bottom Trim
HEADBOARD		
Qty	Dimensions	Description
2	2 ¼ x 2 ¼ x 45 ¼	Legs
2	3/4 x 3 ¾ x 55 ⅛	Rails
2	3/4 x 3 ¼ x 10 (1/2 TBE*)	Outer Stiles
2	3/4 x 2 ½ x 10 (1/2 TBE*)	Inner Stiles
3	1/4 x 9 ⅞ x 15 ½	Panels
1	3/4 x 6 x 55 ⅛ (3/4 TBE*)	Mattress Rail
1	3/4 x 3 x 59 ⅝	Top
1	5/16 x 1 ⅛ x 53 ⅝	Trim
*TBE= Tenon Both Ends		
SIDE RAILS		
Qty	Dimensions	Description
2	3/4 x 6 x 76	Rails
Qty	Dimensions	Description
2	3/4 x 1 x 76 (POPLAR)	Slat Supports
5	3/4 x 2 ½ x 55 (POPLAR)	Slats
HARDWARE		
Qty	Dimensions	Description
1 lb	#6 x 1 ⅝	Wood Screws
1 lb	#6 x 1 ¼	Wood Screws
8	3/8 x 1	Dowel Pins
4	3/8 -16 x 3	Hanger Bolts
4	3/8	Flat washers
4	3/8 -16	Nuts
4	Bed Bolt Covers (Horton Brasses # BC-9; light antique finish)	

Construction

◆Using the dado cutter set in your table saw, set the cutter at 1/4″ wide x 1/2″ deep. Cut a test groove in a piece of scrap to make sure the groove is centered.

◆The center stiles will receive grooves on both edges and the end stiles will get a groove only on one edge.

◆Completed grooves in the stiles.

◆Completed grooves in the rails.

◆Install a combination or cross cutting blade in the table saw. Using the stile as a guide, set the blade height to 1/4″ to cut the tenons. The length of the tenon is 1/2″. Always use the miter gauge set at 90 degrees to the fence.

◆Second cut.

◆Make successive cuts to nibble away at the end of the stile to form the tenon.

◆First cut.

◆Make successive cuts to nibble away at the end of the stile to form the tenon.

◆Lay out the stiles, rails, and panels. Dry fit the assembly before gluing.

◆Apply glue only to the tenons and the area in the groove where they will be positioned. Assemble and clamp at each stile and rail intersection. The panels should be free floating. Set aside to dry.

LEGS

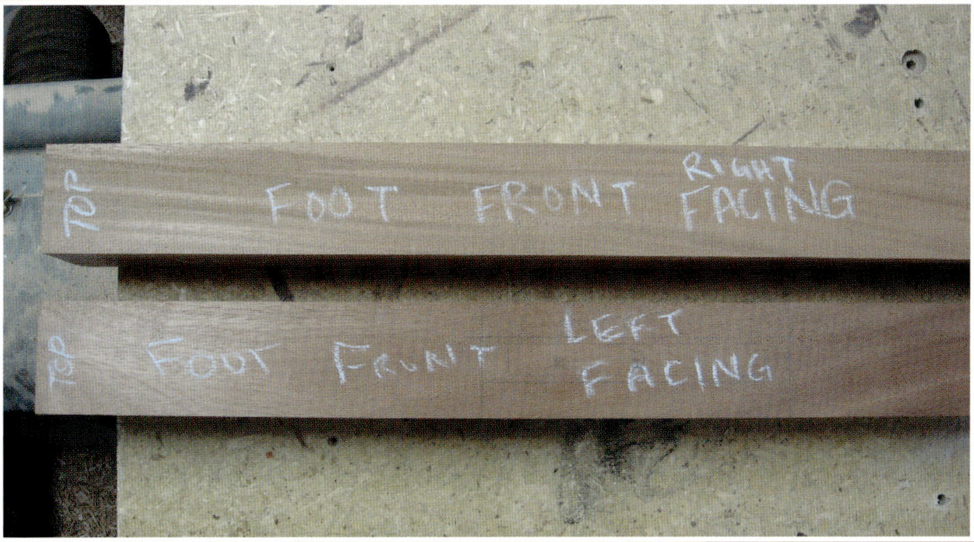

◆Select the face of the leg you want to see when facing the bed and mark. Rotate the legs away from each other and mark for the grooves. Install the dado cutter in the table saw and set at 1/4″ wide x 3/4″ deep. Mark the fence where the blade first comes in contact with the wood.

◆Using a test piece, make sure the groove is centered on the leg.

◆Cut a groove in each of the legs stopping at 15 inches from the top for the footboard and 16-1/2 inches from the top for the headboard.

◆Finished grooves in the legs.

◆Move to the drill press. Make a jig as shown to provide a back fence and stop.

◆Drill the 3/8″ through hole in each leg.

◆Without moving the jig, change to 7/8″ Forstner bit and drill 3/4″ deep.

◆Completed holes.

◆Move back to the table saw and taper the legs using a tapering jig. Sand the tapered areas to remove any saw marks.

◆With 1/4″ wide dado blade installed, set the height to 1/16″. Cut the shallow groove in the bottom of each leg.

◆Completed the cut around the leg.

◆Move to router table. With a 3/8″ core box bit, cut the cove cut into each leg.

◆The finished cut.

◆Using double stick tape, lay the template on each leg. (see template at left)

Footboard Template

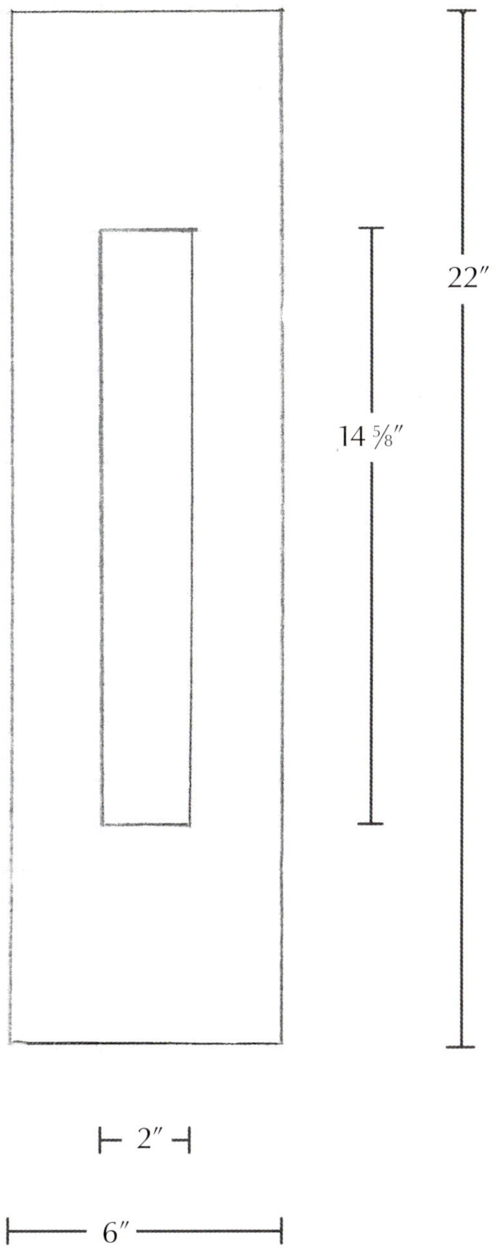

Headboard Template

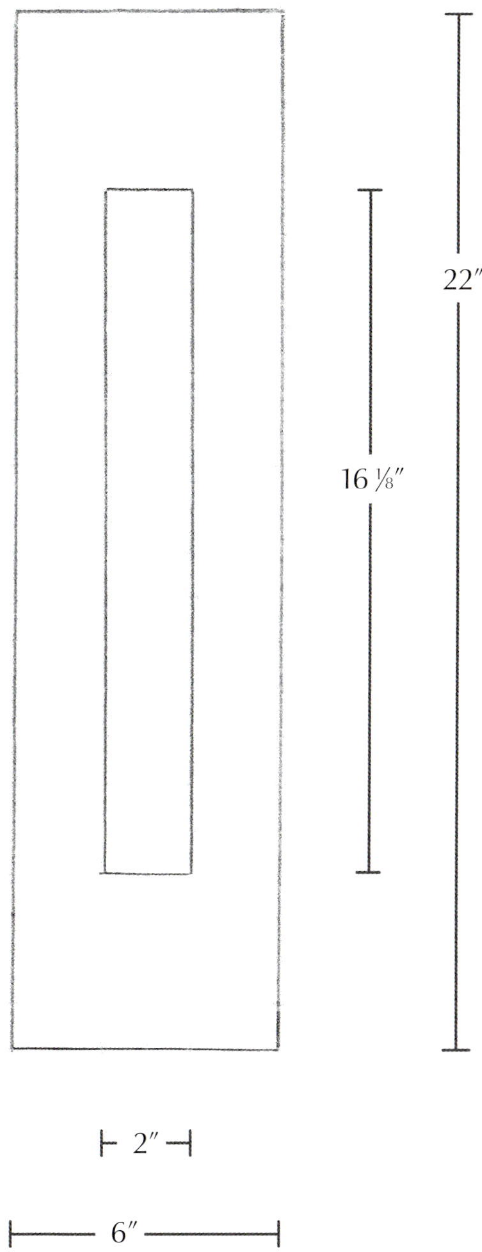

◆Install at 1/4" diameter straight cutting bit and a 3/8" bushing in the router. Follow the outside edge of the template and gradually clean out the center in successive passes.

◆Completed recess after routing.

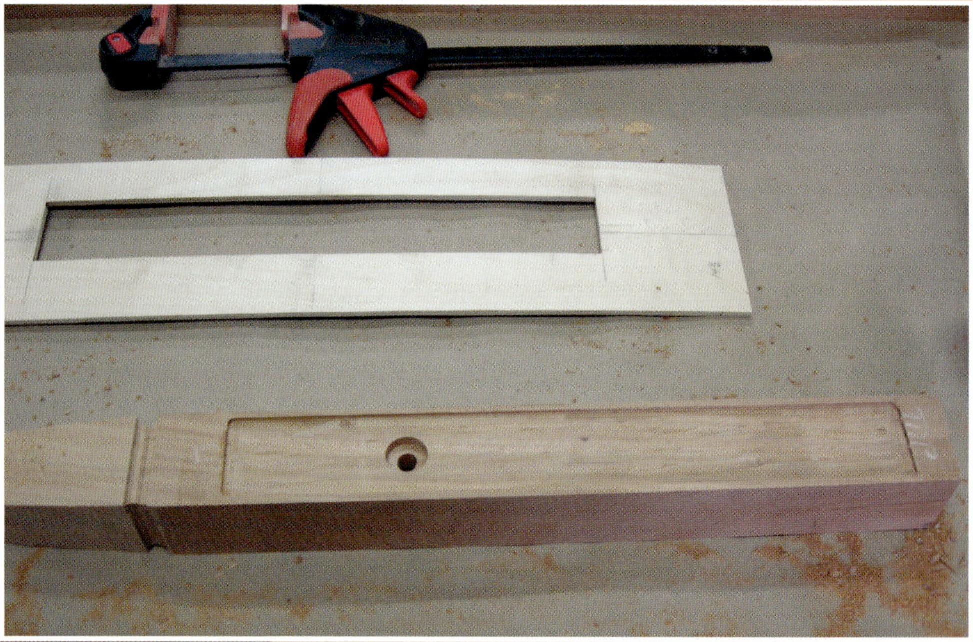

◆At times, homemade tools just work best. This is my version of a sanding block. It measures 1" thick by 4" long x 1-7/8" wide. The clips came from my local office supply store and are stapled in place.

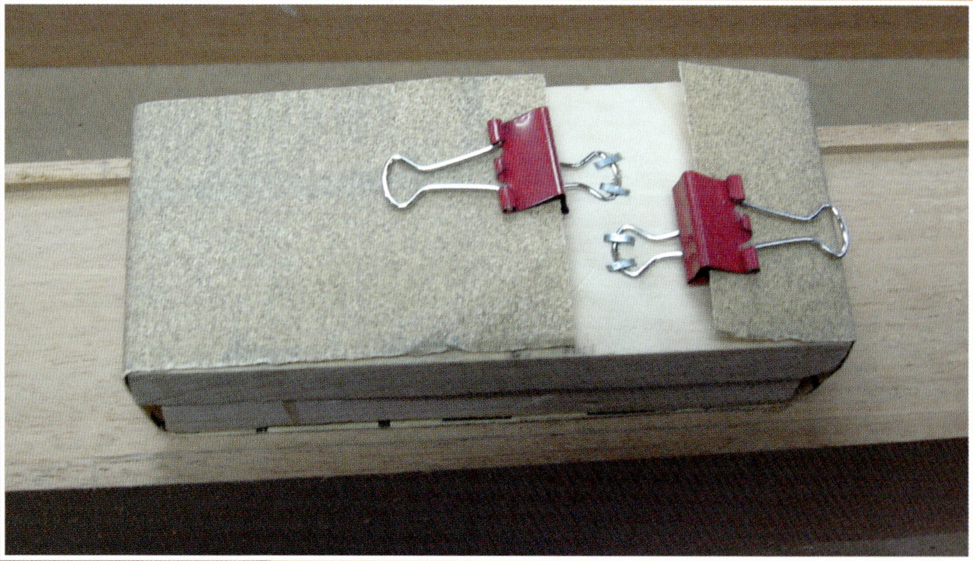

◆Sand the routed area smooth starting with 150 grit and working to 220 grit.

◆Back at the router table, with a 3/16″ roundover bit, route the edges of the leg taper.

◆Install MLCS #6430 groove cutter in the router table. Clamp a stop block to the router fence left of the bit. Set the fence 3/8″ from the center of the bit.

◆Rout the grooves.

◆Move the stop block to the right side of the bit and rout the other side of the grooves to form the corner beads.

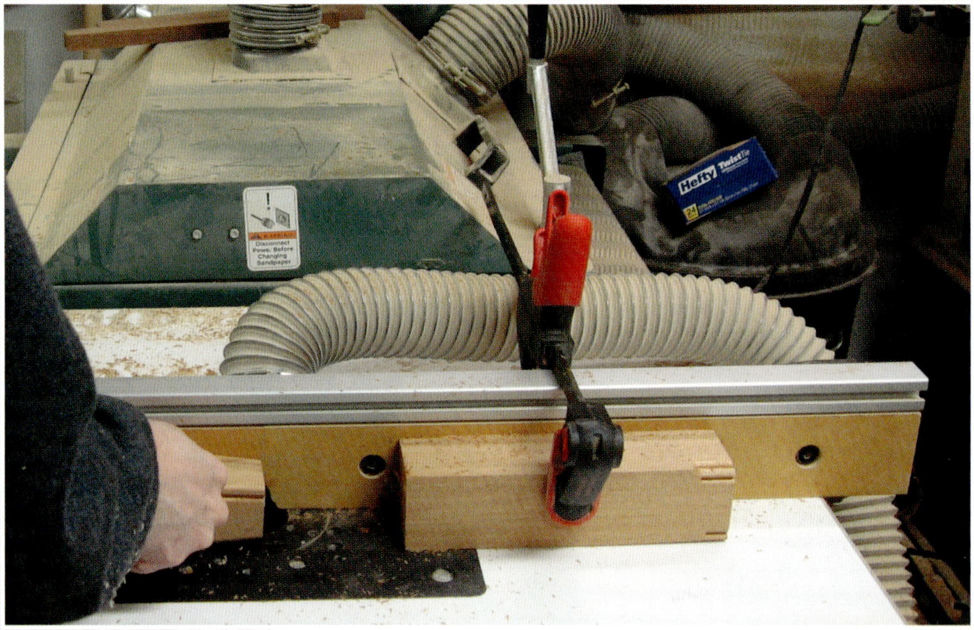

◆Cut the mortises in the headboard legs.

◆Skip cut as shown, keeping a distance between each hole slightly less than 1/4″.

◆Finish cutting the mortise by chiseling between the previously cut holes.

◆Completed mortise.

◆Front view of the completed legs.

◆"Inside" view of completed legs. This will be the side where the panel assembly will be attached.

With a self centering dowel jig, drill the 3/8″ holes 1/2″ deep for the side rail alignment pins. These holes will be on the fronts of the headboard legs and the back of the footboard legs.

◆Completed alignment holes.

◆*Remove the headboard and footboard panel assemblies from the clamps.* Sand the joints flush with a belt sander equipped with 120 grit sandpaper.

◆Finish sanding the assembled panels with a random orbit sander using 150 grit sandpaper, then 220 grit sandpaper

◆Center the flat panels and pin nail in the middle of each end into the stiles.

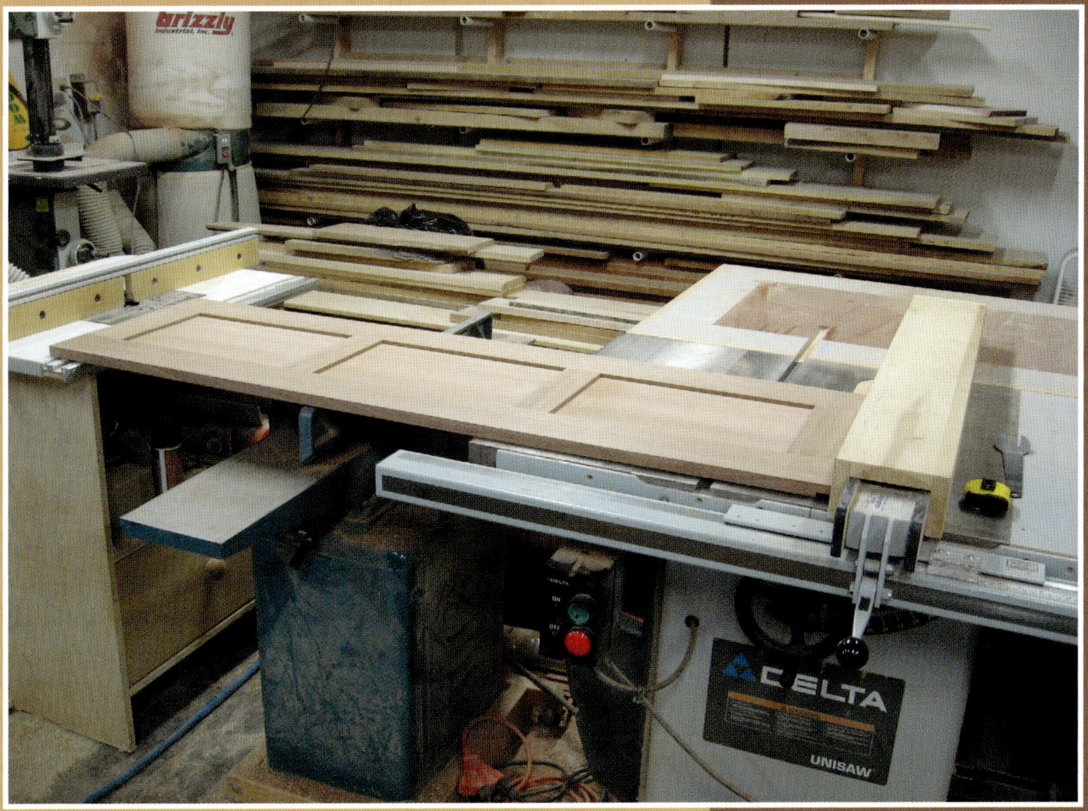

◆Making tenons on the table saw is a challenge with long pieces. Supporting the piece is important. As shown in these pictures, the router table top is the same height as the table saw.

◆Set dado cutter to 1/4″ high and 1/2″ wide. Make the first cut of the 3/4″ long tenon for the head and foot boards.

◆Flip over and cut the other side to form the tenon.

◆With a jigsaw, round the bottom edge of the tenon to fit the groove made with the table saw in each leg.

◆While the table saw is set up with the dado cutter, cut the tenon on the headboard mattress support rail.

◆Raise the blade to 1/2″ high and cut the bottom and top of the tenon.

◆Glue the legs to the panel assembly keeping the top flush.

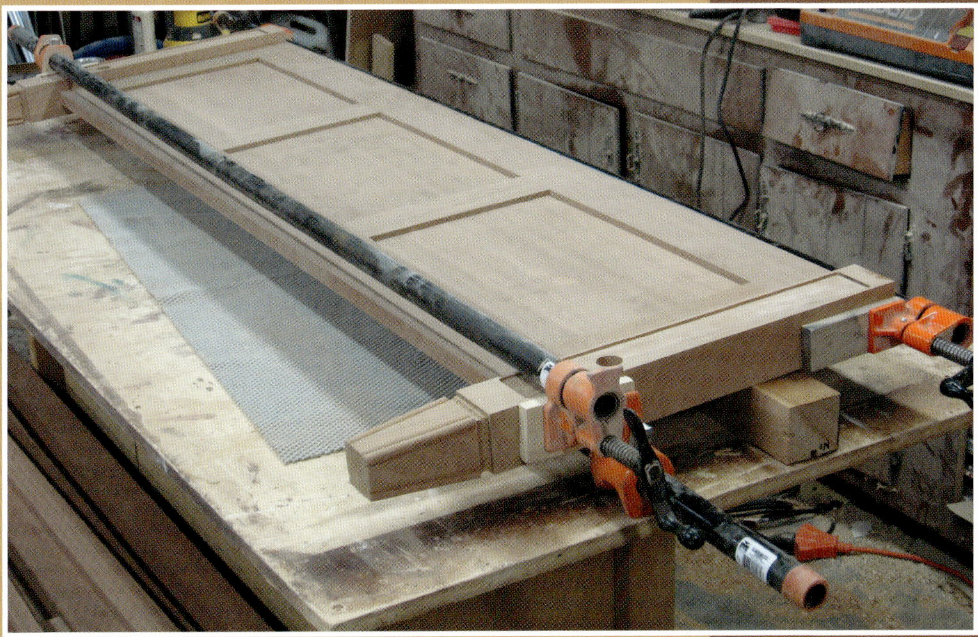

◆Clamp the footboard assembly.

◆Glue together the headboard.

◆Apply clamps to hold joints together.

◆Cut the "notch" into the footboard top using a jigsaw and a straight edge as a guide.

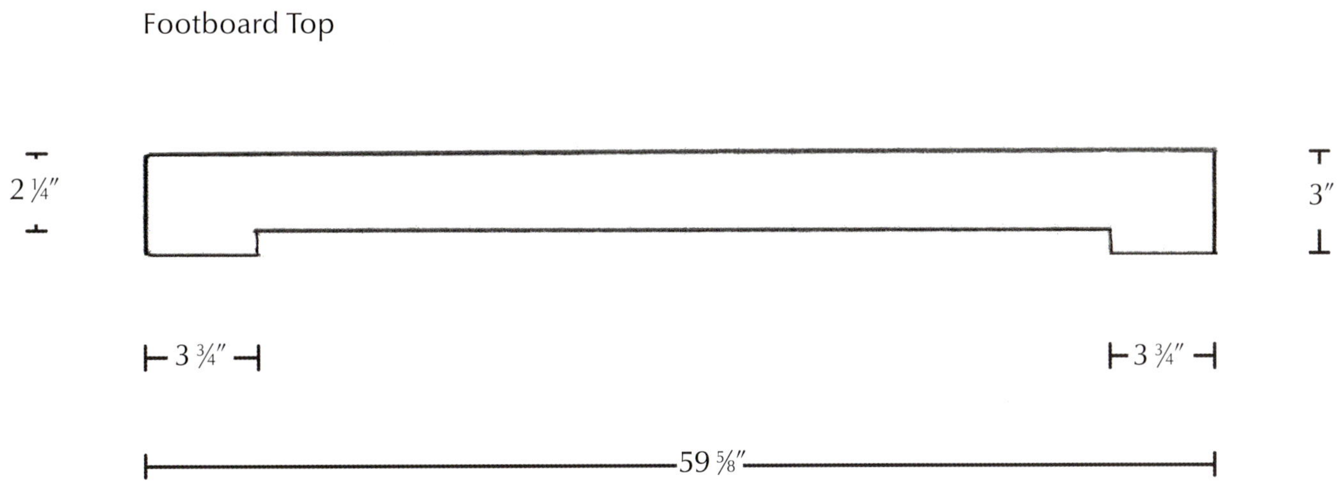

◆Completed cut for the footboard top.

◆Rout the footboard and headboard tops with an ogee profile bit, ends first.

◆Rout the tops lengthwise (use a filler piece as the footboard top is being milled)

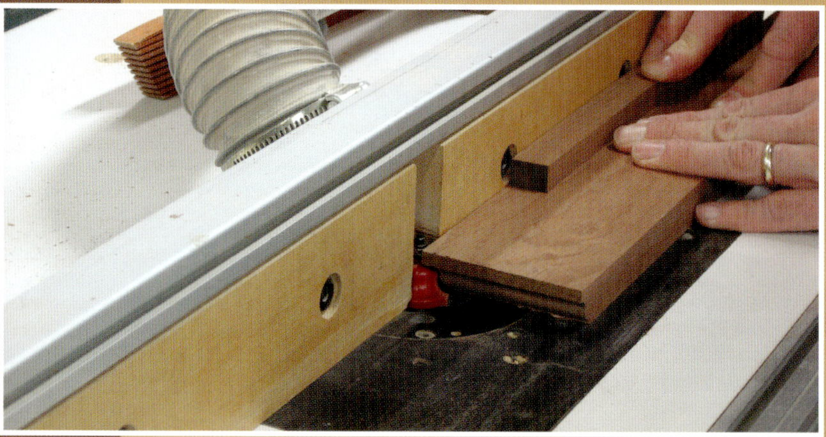

◆Remove the fence and freehand the inside corners of the footboard top.

◆Completed footboard top.

Attach riser blocks to the biscuit joiner so the cuts will be centered at 1-1/8″ high.

◆Cut #20 biscuit slots to accept the tops in the head and foot board assemblies. The biscuit placement is 2-1/4″, 11-1/4″, 23-1/4″, 35-1/4″, 47-1/4″, and 55-7/8″.

◆Stand the tops on their edges and cut the biscuit slots.

◆Completed biscuit cuts.

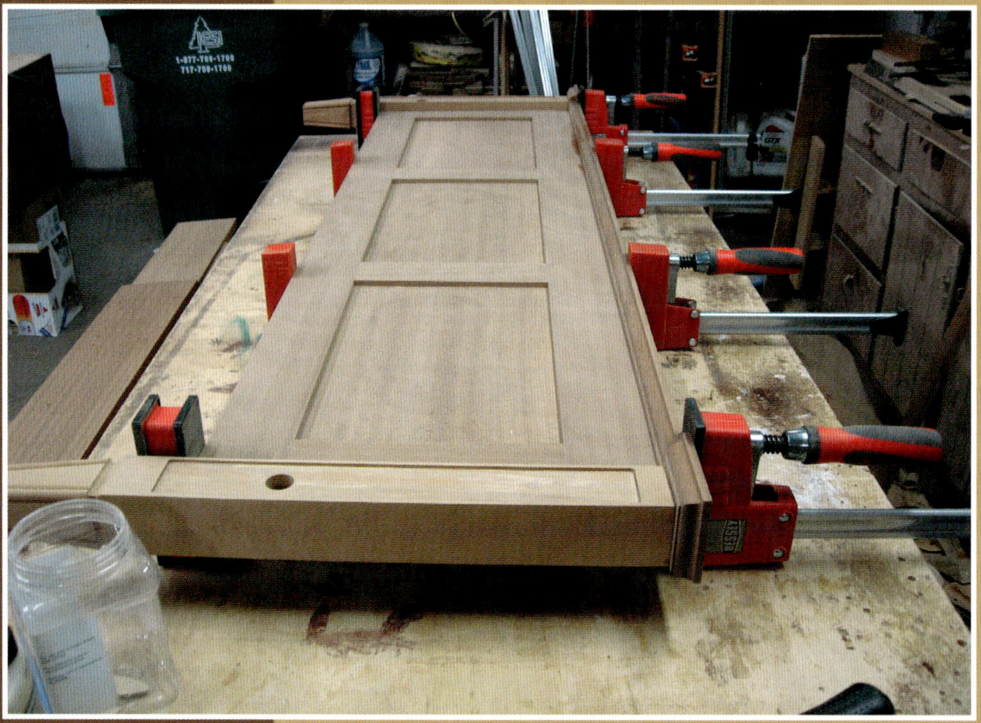

◆Attach the top to the footboard assembly with glue and #20 biscuits and clamp.

◆Glue in #20 biscuits and clamp to the headboard assembly.

◆While the top joint is drying, attach the upper trim with glue on the headboard.

◆Clamp the upper trim with a cowl to provide even pressure along the full length.

◆Make the lower footboard trim at the table saw. This trim is created by setting the dado cutter 1/2″ wide centered on the board. Cut 1/8″ deep.

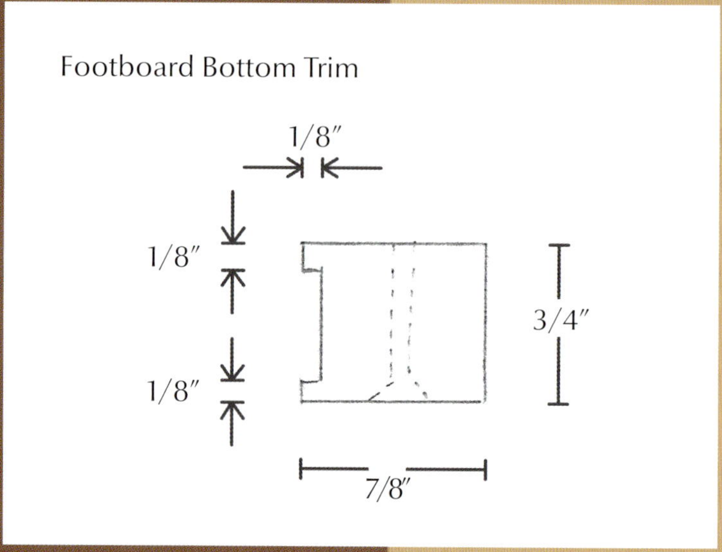

◆Attach the lower footboard trim by pre-drilling and countersinking #6 x 1-1/4″ screws keeping it flush with the back of the panel assembly.

◆Completed footboard trim.

◆After removing the clamps, chisel the corners of the leg recesses square, cutting across the grain first.

◆Clean up the cut.

◆Completed corners.

Side Rails, Top

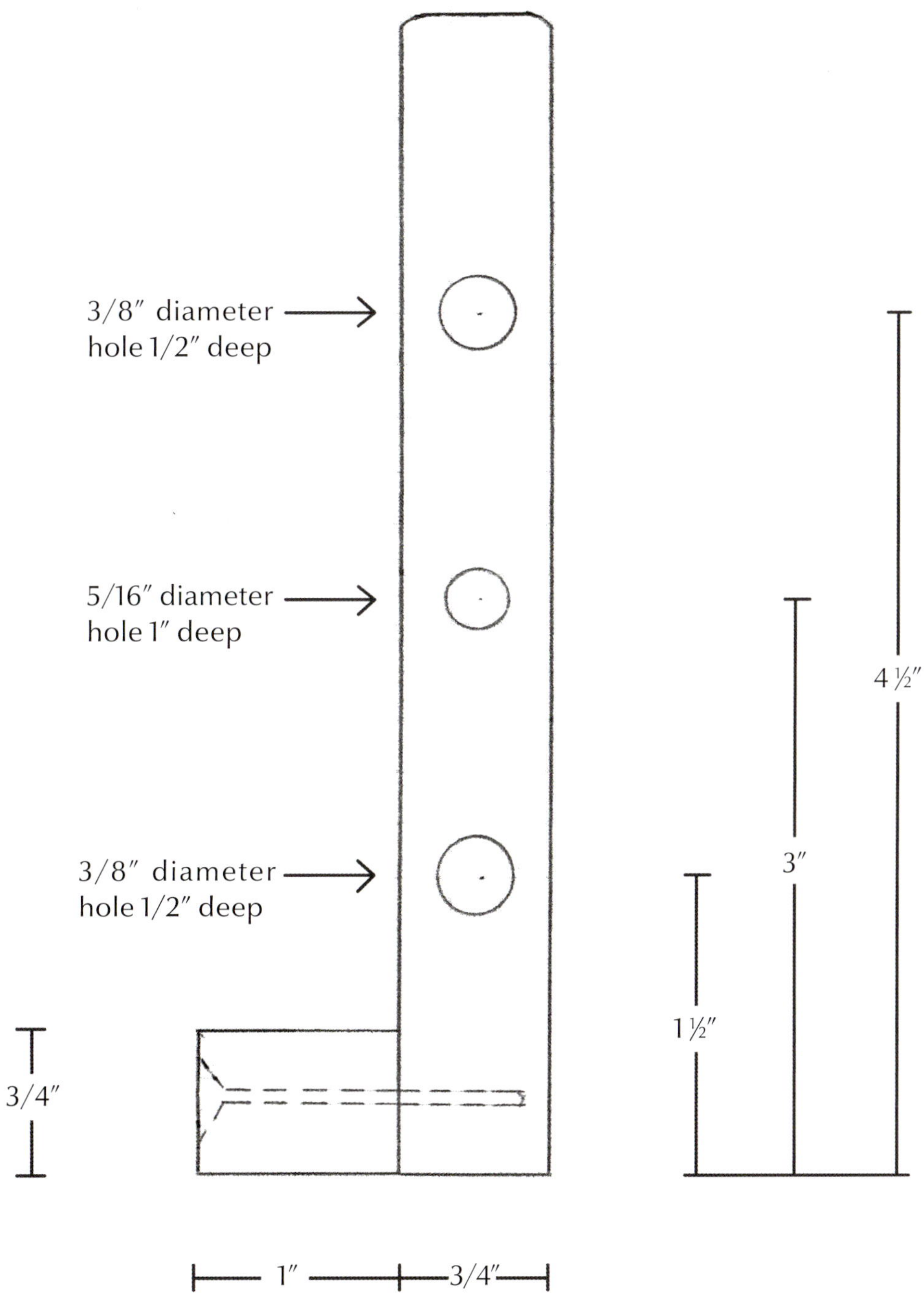

◆Drill two 3/8″ holes 1/2″ deep in each end using a self centering jig.

◆Completed holes.

◆Drill one 5/16″ hole centered in each end to receive the hanger bolt.

◆Completed holes.

◆Install the hanger bolt by screwing in the lag bolt end, allowing 2″ of the bolt threads to protrude.

◆Ease the top edges of the bed rails with 1/4″ roundover bit set at 1/8″ depth of cut.

◆Completed side rail. The dowel pins can now be glued into place.

◆Pre-drill the mattress support runners 1″ from each end and then 9-1/4″ apart throughout the length to accept the #6 x 1-5/8″ wood screws.

◆Using 1-5/8″ screws, attach the runners to the side rails.

◆Completed bed.

Finishing

The finish used on this project was Bartley Pennsylvania Cherry gel stain. Two coats of satin polyurethane were sprayed for lasting protection of the stain. Spray the first coat. When dry, sand with 400 grit paper. Wipe with a tack cloth and spray on the second coat.

◆Plans for King, Queen, and Twin beds.

King Size

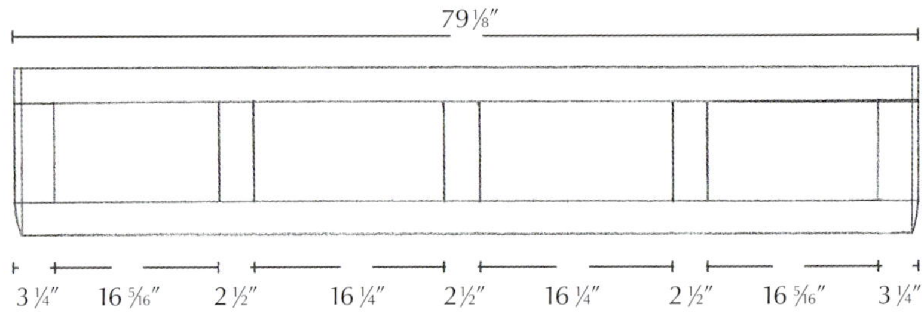

Footboard

2 - 2 ¼″ x 2 ¼″ x 21 ¼″	legs
2 - 3/4″ x 3″ x 79 ⅛″	rails
2 - 3/4″ x 3 ¼″ x 10″	outer stiles
3 - 3/4″ x 2 ½″ x 10″	inner stiles
4 - 1/4″ x 9 ⅞″ x 17 ¼″	panels
1 - 3/4″ x 3″ x 83 ⅝″	top
1 - 3/4″ 1″ x 77 ⅝″	bottom trim

Headboard

2 - 2 ¼″ x 2 ¼″ x 45 ¼″	legs
2 - 3/4″ x 3 ¾″ x 79 ⅛″	rails
2 - 3/4″ 3 ¼″ x 10″	outer stiles
3 - 3/4″ x 2 ½″ x 10″	inner stiles
4 - 1/4″ x 9 ⅞″ x 17 ¼″	panels
1 - 3/4″ x 3″ x 83 ⅝″	top
1 - 5/16″ x 1 ⅛″ 77 ⅝″	trim
1 - 3/4″ x 6″ x 79 ⅛″	mattress rail

Side Rails
2 - 1 ¼″ x 6″ x 81″

Mattress Supports (Poplar)

2 - 1″ x 1″ x 81″	slat supports
4 - 3/4″ x 3″ x 79″	slats
1 - 3/4″ x 3″ x 79 ⅛″	(center slat)
1 - 2 ¼″ x 2 ¼″ x 6″	(center slat support leg)
1 - 1″ x 3″ x 81″	center slat support

King Size Slats & Support Leg

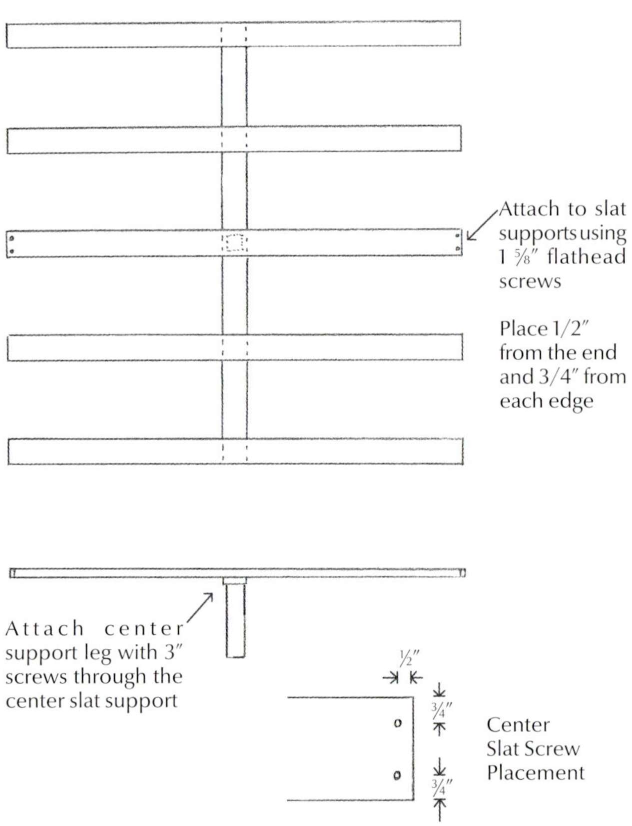

King Size Side Rails, Top

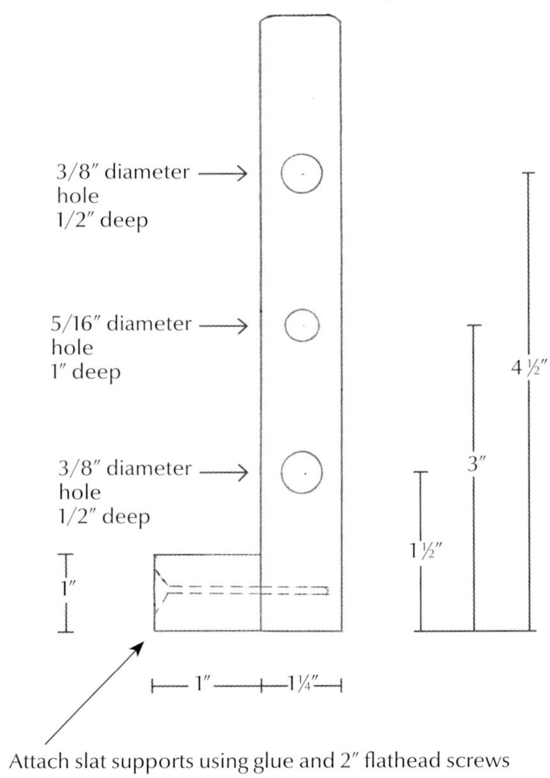

Queen Size

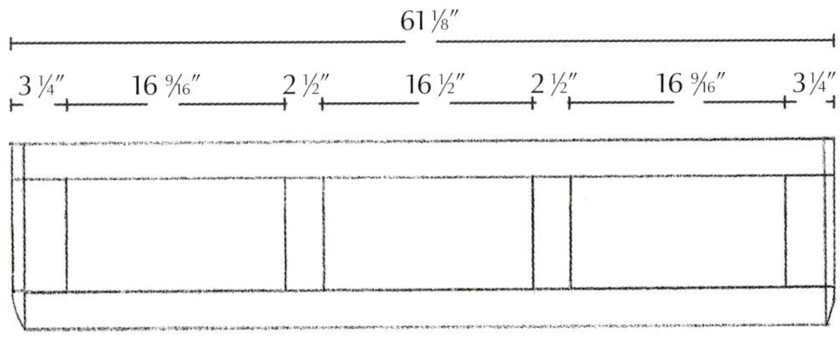

Footboard		Headboard	
2 - 2 1/4″ x 2 1/4″ x 2 1/4″	legs	2 - 2 1/4″ x 2 1/4″ x 45 1/4″	legs
2 - 3/4″ x 3″ x 61 1/8″	rails	2 - 3/4″ x 3 3/4″ x 61 1/8″	rails
2 - 3/4″ x 3 1/4″ x 10″ (1/2″ TBE)	outer stiles	2 - 3/4″ x 3 1/4″ x 10″ (1/2″ TBE)	outer stiles
2 - 3/4″ x 2 1/2″ x 10″ (1/2″ TBE)	inner stiles	2 - 3/4″ x 2 1/2″ x 10″ (1/2″ TBE)	inner stiles
3 - 1/4″ x 9 7/8″ x 17 1/2″	panels	3 - 1/4″ x 9 7/8″ x 17 1/2″	panels
1 - 3/4″ x 3″ x 65 5/8″	top	1 - 3/4″ x 6″ x 61 1/8″ (3/4″ TBE)	mattress rail
1 - 3/4″ x 1″ x 59 5/8″	bottom trim	1 - 3/4″ x 3″ x 65 5/8″	top
		1 - 5/16″ x 1 1/8″ x 59 5/8″	trim

Side Rails
2 - 1″ x 6″ x 81″

Mattress Supports (poplar)
2 - 1″ x 1″ x 81″ slat supports
5 - 3/4″ x 2 1/2″ x 61″ slats

Queen Size Side Rails, top

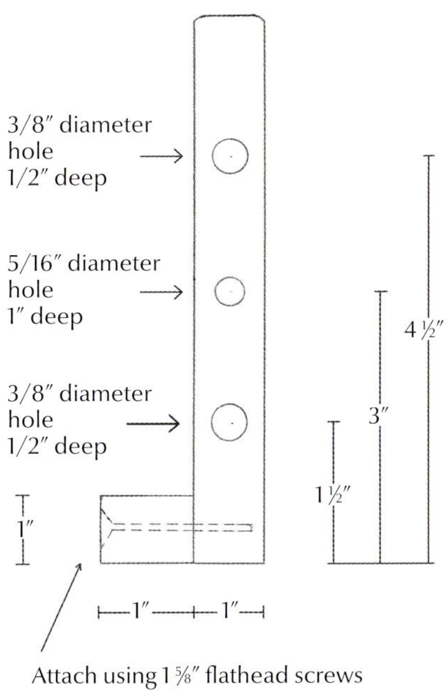

Twin Size

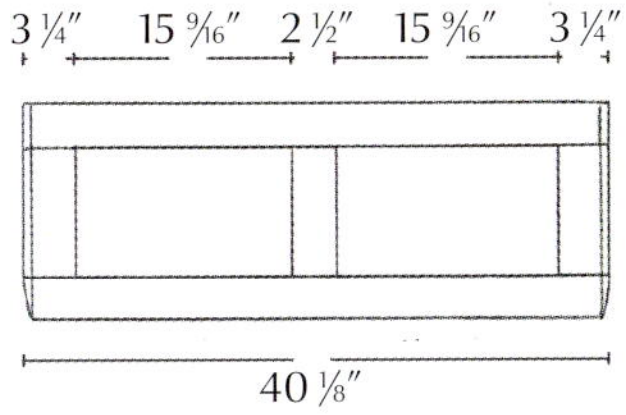

Footboard Dimensions
2 - legs, 2 1/4″ x 2 1/4″ x 2 1/4″
2 - rails, 3/4″ x 3″ x 40 1/8″ (3/4″ TBE)
2 - panels, 1/4″ x 9 7/8″ x 16 1/2″
1 - top, 3/4″ x 3″ x 44 5/8″
1 - bottom trim, 3/4″ x 1″ x 38 5/8″
1 - inner stile, 3/4″ x 2 1/2″ x 10″ (1/2″ TBE)
2 - outer stiles, 3/4″ x 3 1/4″ x 10″ (1/2″ TBE)

Headboard Dimensions
2 - legs, 2 1/4″ x 2 1/4″ x 45 1/4″
2 - rails, 3/4″ x 3 3/4″ x 40 1/8″
2 - panels, 1/4″ x 9 7/8″ x 16 1/2″
1 - top, 3/4″ x 3″ x 44 5/8″
1 - trim, 5/16″ x 1 1/8″ x 38 5/8″
1 - mattress rail, 3/4″ x 6″ x 55 1/8″ (3/4″ TBE)
1 - inner stile, 3/4″ x 2 1/2″ x 10″ (1/2″ TBE)
2 - outer stiles, 3/4″ x 3 1/4″ x 10″ (1/2″ TBE)

Side Rails
2 - 3/4″ x 6″ x 76″

Mattress Supports (poplar)
2 - 3/4″ x 1″ x 76″ slat supports
5 - 3/4″ x 2 1/2″ x 40″ slats

Building the English Style Armoire

Introduction

Building the armoire is both challenging and rewarding. Being a large piece of furniture, it is sure to command attention in any room. Both the subtle details of the tapered and beaded legs and the slight recess on the faces of the legs and drawer dividers lend the armoire a simple elegance. Although designed to complement the bed, this armoire could also be used to house your living room television. Most of the joinery is accomplished at the table saw using a dado blade and a standard blade. Details are made with a trim router and both handheld and table mounted routers.

Armoire Cut List (listed in inches)

Qty	Dimensions	Description	Wood Type
1	3/4 x 20 x 46	Top	Mahogany
4	1¾ x 1¾ x 71¼	Legs	Mahogany
2	3/4 x 3¾ x 16½ (1″ TBE*)	Top Side Rails	Mahogany
2	3/4 x 2 x 16½ (1″ TBE*)	Mid Side Rails	Mahogany
2	3/4 x 2 x 16½ (1″ TBE*)	Bottom Side Rails	Mahogany
2	1/2 x 15 x 26⅛	Top Side Panels	Mahogany
2	1/2 x 15 x 32⅞	Bottom Side Panels	Mahogany
1	3/4 x 16 7/16 x 40¼	Inner Shelf	Mahogany
1	3/4 x 3¾ x 38½	Top Front Rail	Mahogany
1	3/4 x 1½ x 38½	Intermediate Front Rail	Mahogany
2	3/4 x 2 x 38½	Bottom Front Rail	Mahogany
3	3/4 x 2¾ x 40¼	Drawer Dividers	Mahogany
1	3/4 x 2 x 40¼	Bottom Rail Support	Mahogany
1	3/4 x 3 x 59⅝	Top	Mahogany
2	3/4 x 3 x 48	Molding Blanks	Mahogany
2	1/8 x 1 x 14½	Top Molding Backer	Mahogany
1	1/8 x 1 x 38½	Top Molding Backer	Mahogany
2	1/8 x 2 x 1¾	Bottom Rear Leg Trim	Mahogany
1	1/8 x 2 x 12 (CTF*)	Bottom Front Leg Trim	Mahogany
2	1/8 x 2¼ x 1¾	Top Rear Leg Trim	Mahogany
1	1/8 x 2¼ x 12 (CTF*)	Top Front Leg Trim	Mahogany
4	3/4 x 1⅜ x 14½	Pocket Door Slides Backing	Mahogany
2	3/4 x 3 x 20	Pocket Door Follower Strips	Mahogany
1	3/4 x 5¾ x 40½ (1″ TBE*)	Top Back Board	Mahogany
4	3/4 x 6 x 40½ (1″ TBE*)	Intermediate Back Boards	Mahogany
1	3/4 x 5½ x 40½ (1″ TBE*)	Bottom Back Board	Mahogany
5	1/4 x 6 7/16 x 39	Back Filler Boards	Mahogany
4	3/4 x 2¼ x 26	Door Stiles	Mahogany
4	3/4 x 2¼ x 15½	Door Rails (3/8″ TBE*)	Mahogany
2	1/2 x 15⅜ x 22¼	Door Panels	Mahogany
1	3/4 x 5 13/16 x 38⅜	Drawer Front	Mahogany
1	3/4 x 6 13/16 x 38⅜	Drawer Front	Mahogany
1	3/4 x 7 13/16 x 38⅜	Drawer Front	Mahogany
1	3/4 x 8 9/16 x 38⅜	Drawer Front	Mahogany
1	3/4 x 5 13/16 x 38⅜	Drawer Back	Poplar
1	3/4 x 6 13/16 x 38⅜	Drawer Back	Poplar
1	3/4 x 7 13/16 x 38⅜	Drawer Back	Poplar
1	3/4 x 8 9/16 x 38⅜	Drawer Back	Poplar
2	5/8 x 5 13/16 x 15	Drawer Sides	Poplar
2	5/8 x 6 13/16 x 15	Drawer Sides	Poplar
2	5/8 x 7 13/16 x 15	Drawer Sides	Poplar
2	5/8 x 8 9/16 x 15	Drawer Sides	Poplar
4	1/2 x 14½ x 37⅝	Drawer Bottoms	Maple Plywood
8	25/32 x 1¼ x 14½	Drawer Guides	Poplar
8	3/4 x 2 x 14¼	Drawer Runners	Poplar
8	1/4 x 3/4 x 2	Drawer Stops	Poplar

*TBE= Tenon Both Ends
*CTF= Cut To Fit

HARDWARE

Qty	Dimensions	Description
1 lb	#7 x 1¼	Pocket Screws
1 lb	#7 x 1½	Pocket Screws
4	Tack Glides # 57.01.05.04 Knapp Vogt Pocket	Custom Service Hardware
2	Door Kit #8070PEZEB16 Knobs #H-46 Light Antique	Custom Service Hardware
8	Brass Finish Bail Pulls #H10FB Light	Horton Brasses
8	Antique Brass Finish Heavy Duty Thumb Tacks	Horton Brasses

Construction

Panels

Begin by gluing up the panels to the required sizes from the cut list. While the panels are drying, cut the remaining parts to the dimensions on the cut list. Labeling each piece as they are cut will make it easier to identify the pieces for the joinery section.

Once the panels are dry, scrape off any glue residue and sand flat. Using the Shaker raised panel cutter with the height set at 1/4", rout the four side panels and the two door panels. This will produce a 1/4" thick by 1/2" deep tongue.

◆Machine the end grain first.

◆Machine with the grain direction.

◆Back view of the panel raise. Sand both sides of the panels at this time so they are ready for the assembly process.

Legs

The legs are the most demanding part of this piece of furniture. Close attention to the details will yield great results.

◆Clearly identify the position of each leg: left front, left rear, right front, and right rear.

◆Mark the faces of each leg that will be seen.

◆Identify what will be the bottom end of each leg.

After identifying where each leg will be located, mark the location of the mortises according to the drawings.

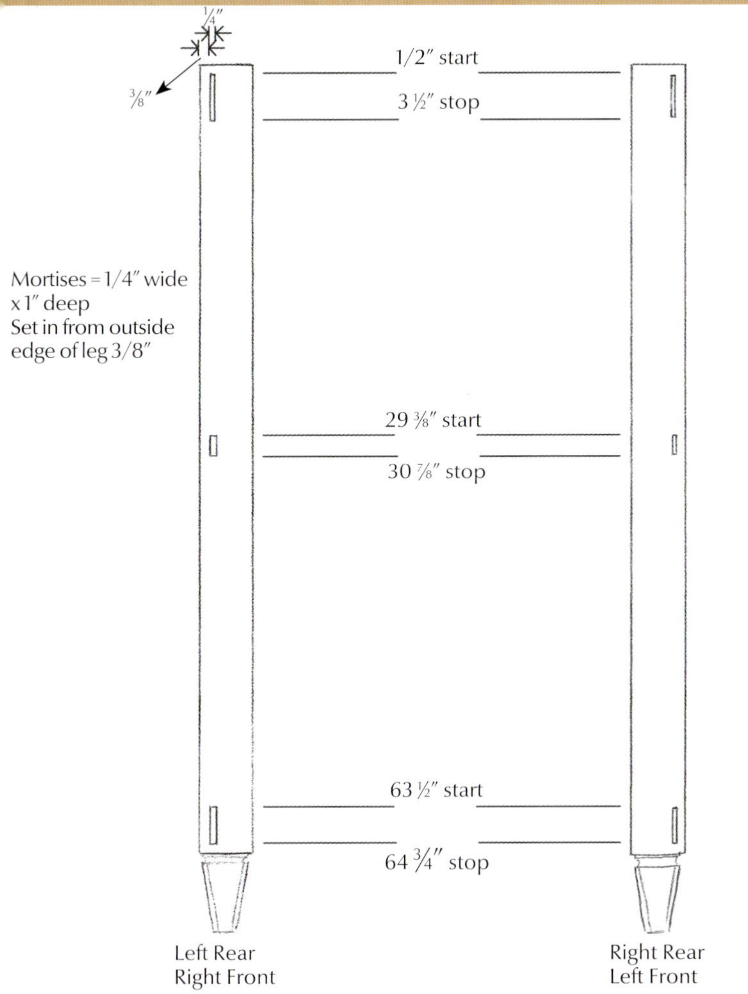

Mortise Placement (measure from top)

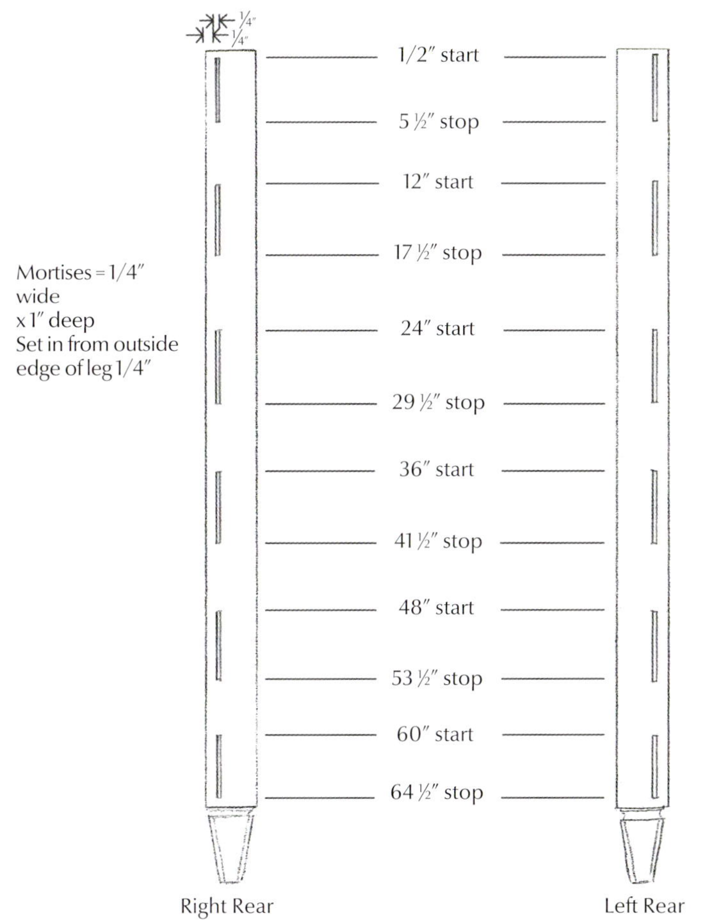

Mortise Placement

◆Install a dado cutter measuring 1/4″ wide into the table saw. Set the height at 3/8″ high and 3/8″ from the fence to form the grooves for the side panels. Mark the end of where the blade touches the wood on the table saw fence.

◆Mark where the blade first touches the wood.

◆Cut the grooves for the side panels stopping at the layout line.

◆Finished grooves for the sides.

◆Adjust the fence to 1/4″ from the dado cutter and lower the blade to 1/4″ high. Cut the grooves for the back.

◆At the mortising machine, cut the 1/4″ wide by 1″ deep mortises for the back boards. The groove will act as a guide for the mortising chisel. Skip a chisel's width between holes. *Note: Mortises can also be made with a drill press equipped with a brad point bit using the same method. The waste can then be removed with a chisel.*

◆Finish cutting the mortise by cleaning out the remaining spaces.

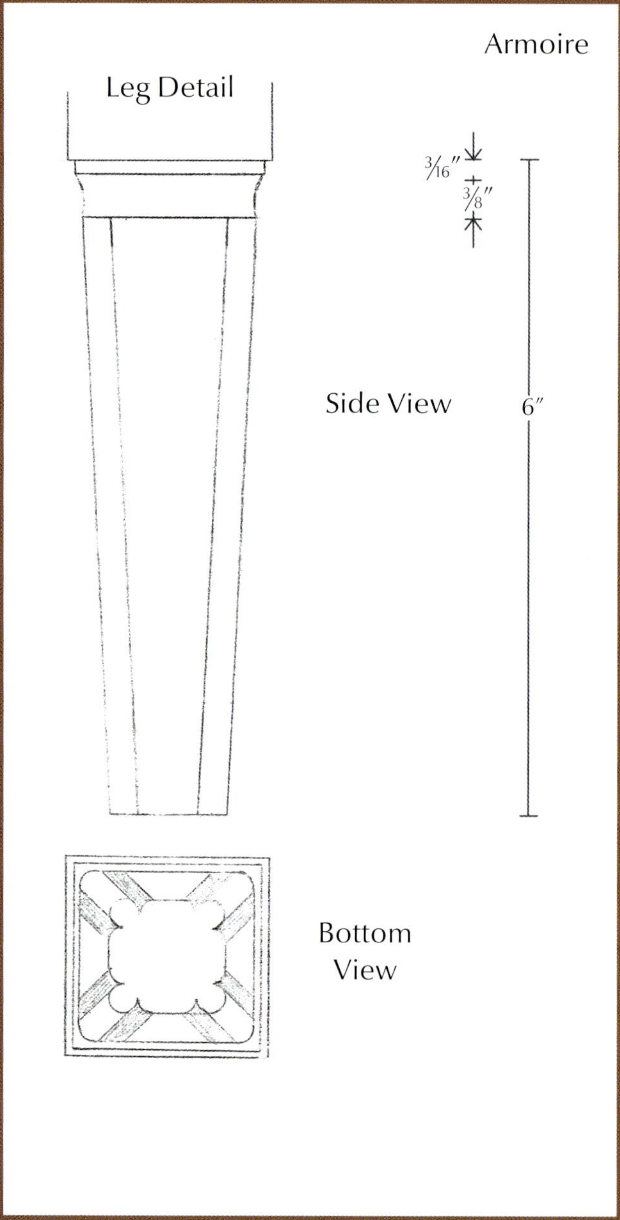

◆***Decorative cuts:***
Begin with the bottom of the legs. With the dado cutter still in the table saw, lower the blade to 1/16″ height. The fence should be set at 6″ away from the far side of the blade. Cross cut each leg on all four sides.

◆Route the cove area with a 1/2″ core box bit and a speed square clamped in place. The bit height should be set at 1/4″ high and will partially remove (less than an 1/8″) some of the dado made in the previous step.

◆Finished cuts.

◆Mark the leg tapers from the edge of the cove to the bottom coming in 3/8″ from the edge. The leg should measure 1″ wide at the bottom.

◆Using a tapering jig, taper all four sides of the legs.

◆One completed leg with tapers.

◆Sand the tapers to prepare for making the grooves.

◆Install an 1/8″ point cutting roundover bit in a trim router with a straight edge guide. The center of the bit should be 3/16″ from the edge guide and 1/8″ deep. Carefully cut the grooves.

◆Finish the beading with a hand plane to round over the outside edges.

◆Finished grooves.

◆End view of the finished beading.

◆Cut the decorative recess in the two front legs with a 1/4″ straight bit and a trim router with a straight edge guide. The depth of cut should be set at 3/32″. Adjust the edge guide to let 3/16″ on the outside edge of the leg. *Notice the straight edge guide is on the far side from the bit.*

◆With a speed square clamped in place, rout across the end of the recess being cautious to stay within the lines.

◆Chisel each of the corners square.

◆The finished corners of the recessed area.

◆Sand the recessed area with a homemade sanding block to remove any marks left by the router.

◆Tap the metal tack glides onto the bottoms of each leg. This will keep the legs off the floor and keep them from splintering when the piece is moved.

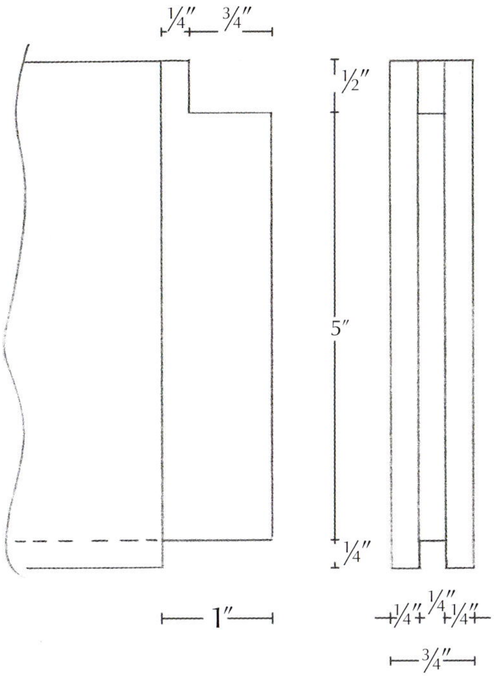

(1) Top Back Board Haunched,
Tenon Both Ends [TBE]

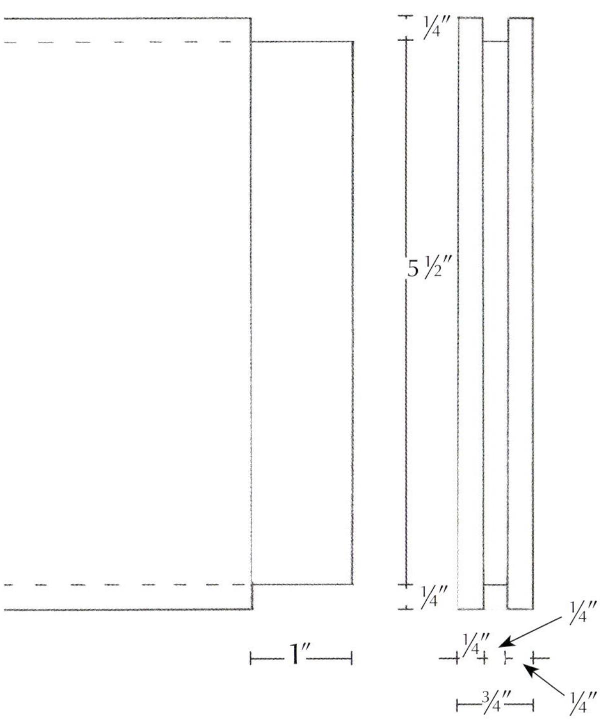

(4) Middle Back Boards,
Tenon Both Ends [TBE]

Making the Tenons

The case work is primarily built using mortise and tenon joinery, while the doors are constructed using tongue and groove joints. The tenons are all made in the same way, just different lengths. With a fine cutting blade installed in the table saw, make the tenons. The blade height should be set to 1/4″ high. Dry fitting into the leg mortises is recommended for a proper fit.

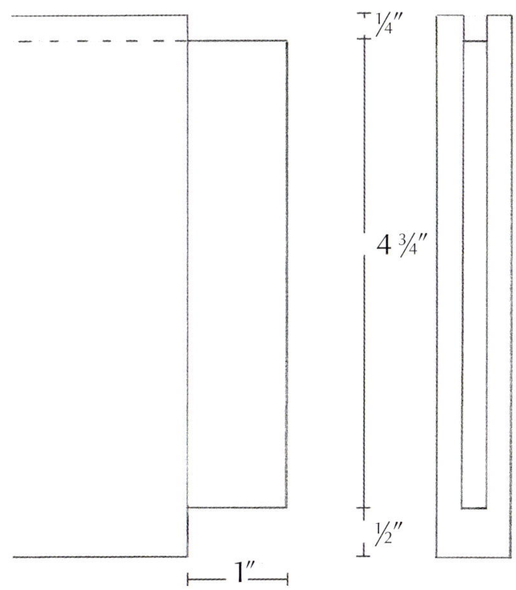

Bottom Back Board,
Tenon Both Ends [TBE]

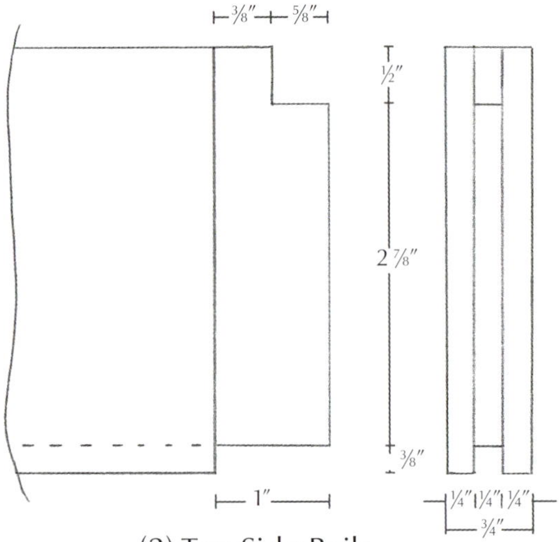

(2) Top Side Rails Haunched, Tenon Both Ends

Middle Side Rails Tenon Both Ends

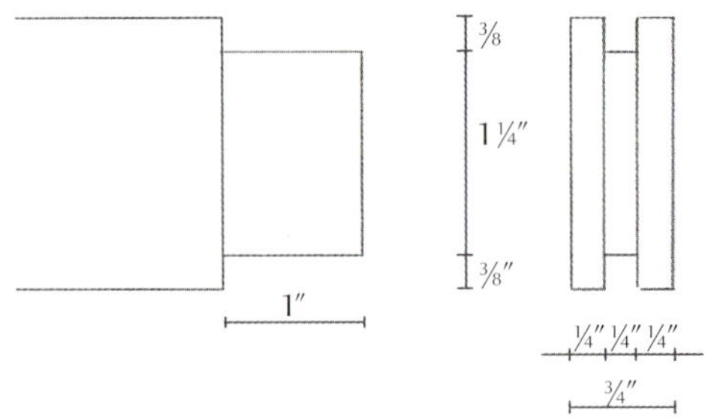

Bottom Side Rails, Tenon Both Ends

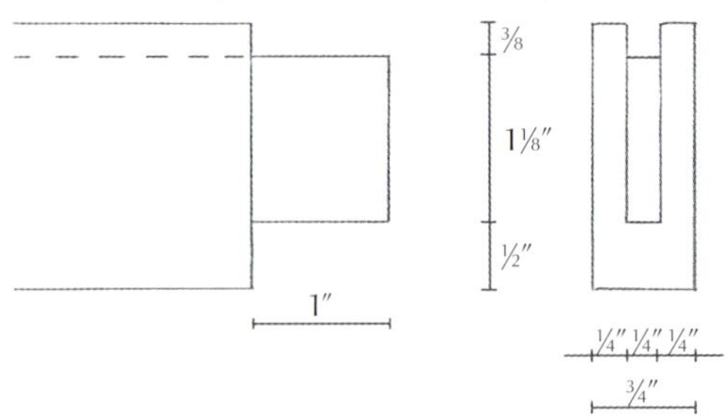

(4) Door Top & Bottom Rails Tenon Both Ends

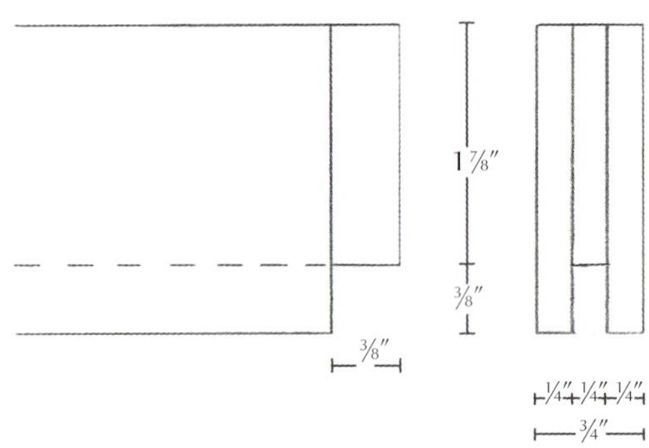

◆Begin by cutting the cheek cut on one side

◆Flip the board over and cut the cheek cut on the other side.

◆Make successive cuts to form the tenon. This could also be done with a dado blade.

◆Install the dado cutter into the table saw and cut the grooves in the door rails and stiles (second shot), the side rails, and the back rails.

Door Construction

◆Lay out the door parts orienting them where they will be placed for assembly.

◆Install the bottom rail into the stile with glue on the tenon and in the mortise.

◆Place panel into the "L" shaped parts—no glue on the panel.

◆Glue the top rail in place.

◆Finish assembling the door by taping the other stile in place.

◆Check that the door is square by measuring from corner to corner and clamp.

◆Center the panel and tack a 5/8″ long brad at the center of each end on the rail to keep the panel centered.

Back

This is the most challenging aspect of the project. Using slow setting glue and dry fitting all of the parts will aid in the assembly process. Sand all parts before gluing together.

Back Board Placement

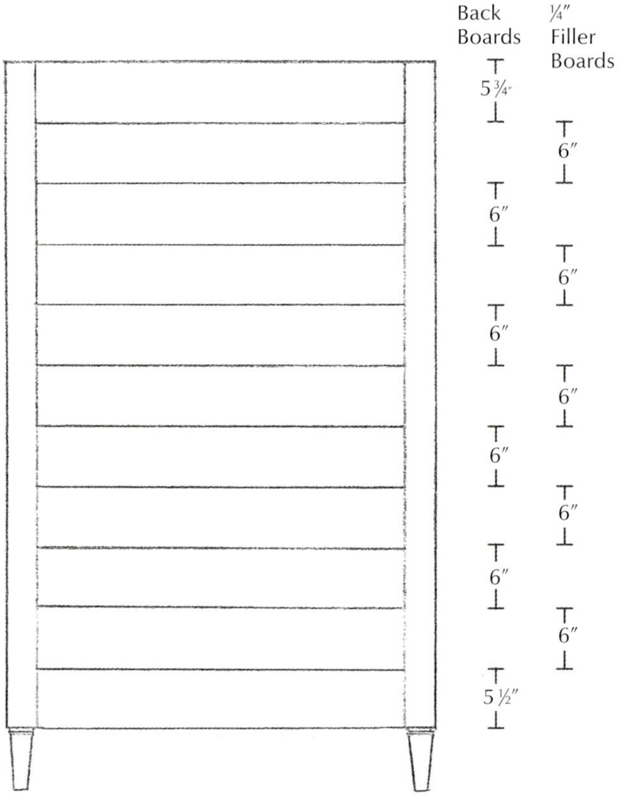

◆Start to assemble the back by clamping one leg to the workbench. Install the top board first, gluing only the mortises and tenons. Alternate the 1/4″ filler boards and back rails in one rear leg.

◆Apply glue into the mortises of the remaining rear leg. Tap the second back leg onto the back boards. Clamp and let dry.

◆Lay the back on the workbench with side mortises up and dry fit the side pieces. Sand the rails. Assembling one side at a time, glue the top rail into place, making sure each rail is square. Place the top panel in the rear leg groove and glue in the mid-rail, making sure it is 29-1/8″ from the top. Do not glue the panels.

◆Clamp the mid- and top rail in place. Install bottom side panel and glue in the bottom rail.

◆The bottom rail will be even with the top of the rabbet cut on the leg. Check for square.

Case Side Assembly

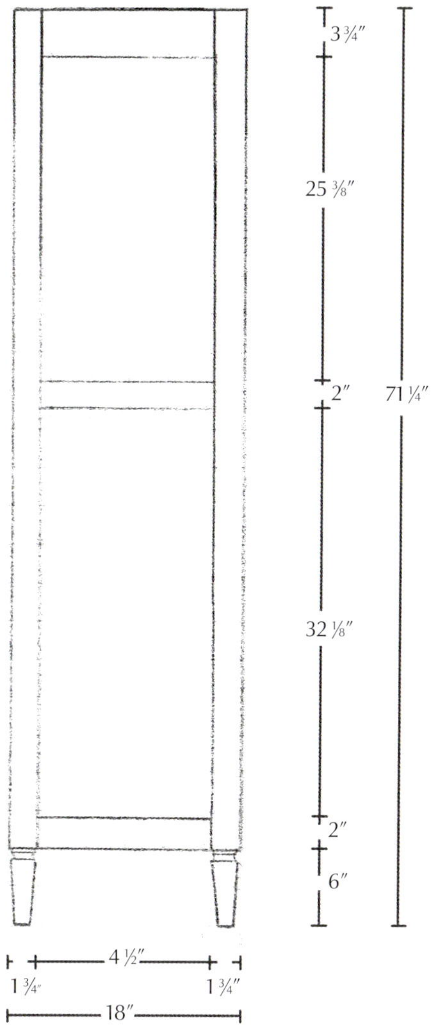

◆Install front leg with glue in the mortises and on the rail tenons. Again, the top should be flush and the bottom rail even with the leg rabbet.

◆Use clamps with blocks to protect the recessed detail on the front legs when clamping the sides together.

◆Center the panels and from the inside shoot 5/8″ brads into the rails to hold them into place.

Front rails

◆Attach a 6″ tall x 24″ long sacrificial fence to the miter gauge. This fence will support the parts and push the cut off pieces past the blade.

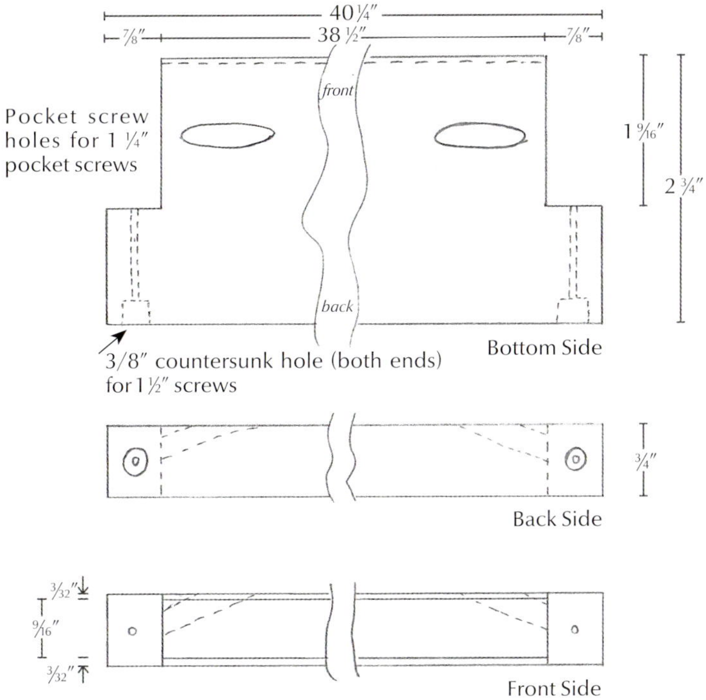

(3) Drawer Dividers

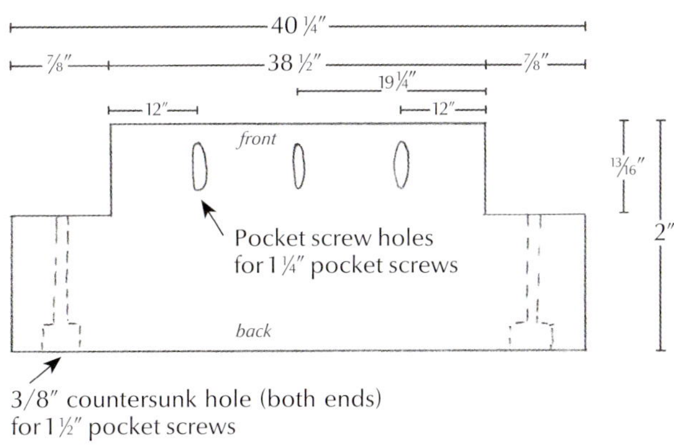

Bottom Drawer Divider Backer

◆Make the first cut with the blade height at 9/16″. Adjust the table saw fence to 1-9/16″ from the far side of the blade.

◆Adjust the table saw fence to 9/16″ from the far side of the blade and 1-9/16″ high

◆Finished drawer divider notch cuts. Adjust the fence and cut the notches for the bottom rail at this time.

◆Cut the notches in the shelf as per the drawing.

Under Side of Shelf

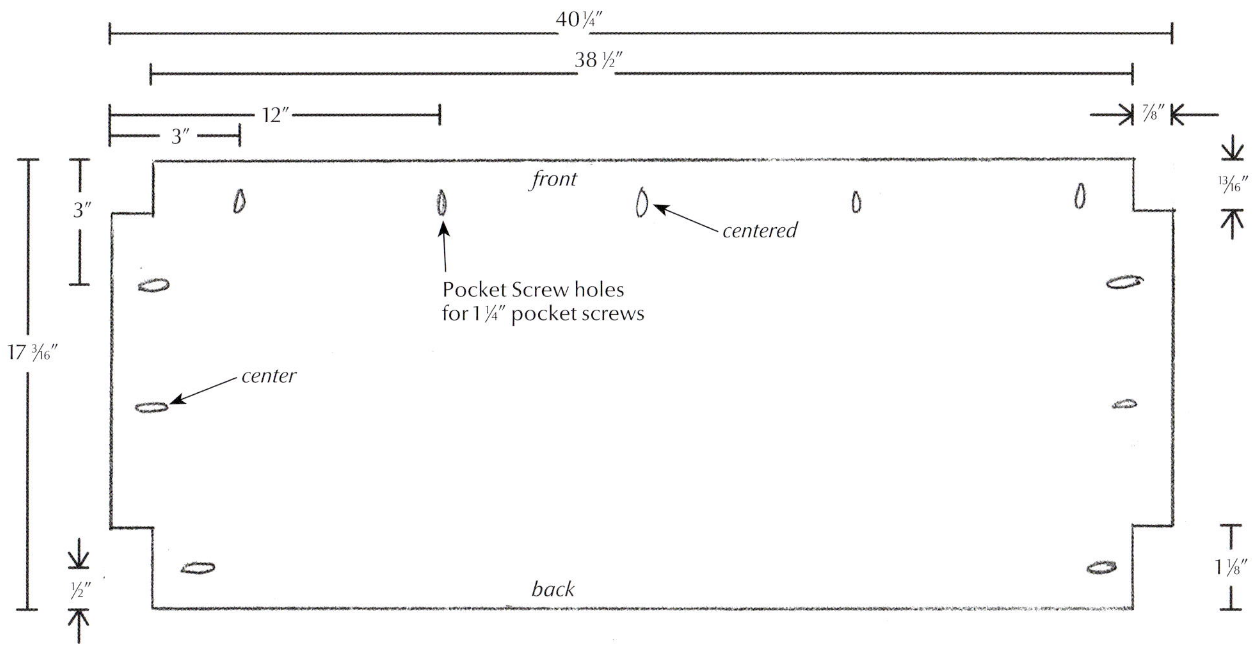

◆Install the dado blade and set it at 9/16″ wide x 1/16″ high. Set the fence 3/32″ from the blade. Machine three drawer dividers to form a dado groove. While the dado cutter is at the proper height and the fence is 3/32″ from the blade. Cut the dado in the 1-1/2″ and 2″ front rails (intermediate and bottom). Clean up any saw marks with 150 grit sandpaper and a sanding block.

◆Drill pocket holes in the 1-3/8″, 2″, and 3-3/4″ rails (1-3/8″ and 2″ rails shown).

◆Drill pocket holes in the (3) drawer dividers per the drawing. Drill a hole with the pocket hole bit on the backside 3/8″ in from the edge to form a countersink 1/4″ deep. Finish drilling through with a 1/8″ bit.

◆Drill the pocket screw holes in the shelf.

Case
Front Rail Placement

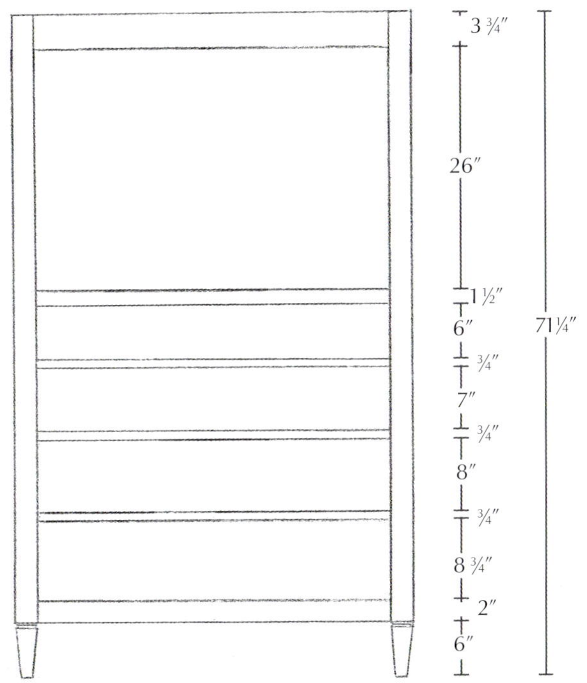

◆Roll the case onto its side and attach the top front rail and bottom front rail using pocket screws. The rail should be recessed 3/16″ from the front of the leg.

◆Attach the front rails using 1-1/4″ pocket hole screws. From the back of the rail, use a 1-1/2″ pocket hole screw in each countersunk hole into the legs.

◆Attach the rail support to the bottom rail, keeping it flush with the top of the 2″ rail.

◆Tap the shelf into place from the bottom by angling it behind the front mid-rail. Keep the front toward the top of the case and the back toward the bottom of the case. The back will fit up against the bottom of the 3rd back board from the top. Screw into the front rail, keeping the shelf flush with the top of the rail.

◆Next, screw into the rear legs, then the side rails. This piece was built during the dry winter months, so an expansion gap is necessary.

Interior Parts

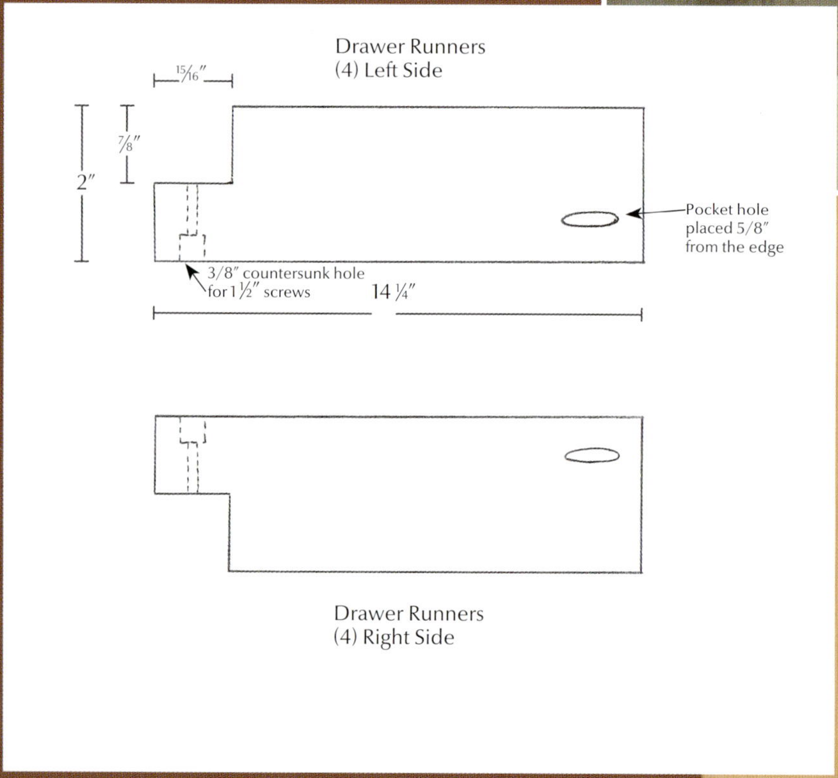

Drawer Openings

◆Notch eight drawer runners and drill the countersunk holes.

◆Drill pocket holes on the opposite side of the notch.

◆Install each of the drawer runners to the front rails. Screw the back of the runners into the legs 1/16″ higher than the front.

◆Install thumbtacks where the drawers will ride, keeping them 1/8″ from the edge of the front rails. This will also space the drawer fronts 1/16″ above the drawer dividers.

Install the top at this time using 1-1/4" pocket screws keeping the back flush. All of the pocket holes should be inside the case. The front and sides will have a 2" overhang.

◆Install eight 3/4" x 1-1/4" x 14-1/2" drawer guides using one 1-1/4" pocket screw in each end to attach to the legs.

◆Install the four pieces of mahogany, 3/4" x 1-3/8" x 14-1/2", for the pocket door slides. Place one on each side of the shelf and attach with 1-1/4" pocket screws into the legs.

◆Attach the top two pocket door slide supports even with the door opening. Use a 3-3/4"spacer to keep the support consistently spaced.

◆Install the drawer stops with glue and 5/8" brads on each of the front rails, keeping them 1" from the legs and 3/4" from the front of the rails.

Molding/ trim

◆Plane filler strips to 1/8″ thick by 1″ wide. Using 5/8″ brads, attach the filler strip 3/4″ from the underside of the top. Use a 3/4″ spacer block to keep thin pieces consistent.

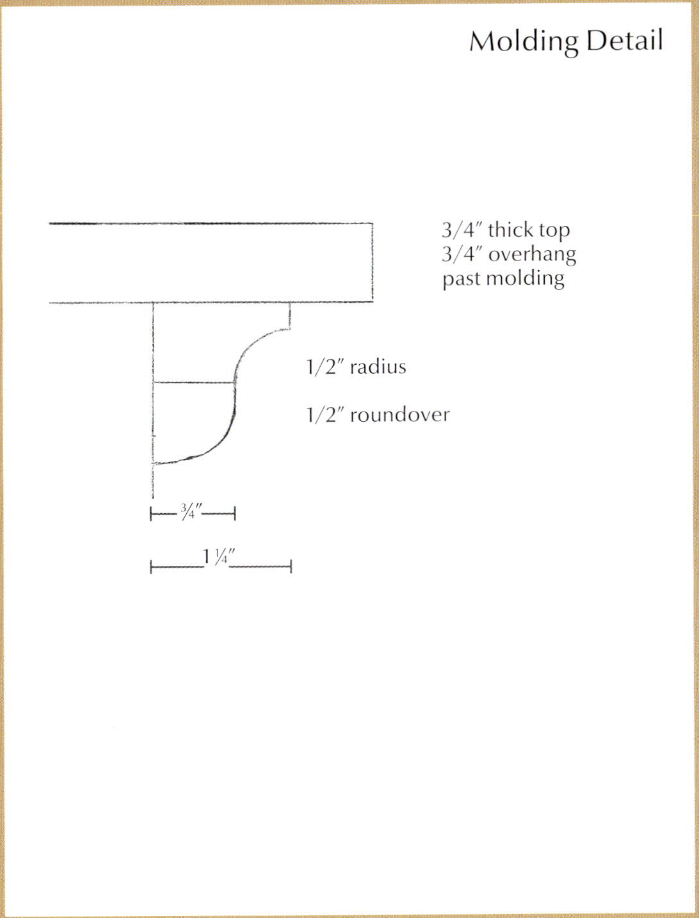

◆Make the top molding from two pieces of mahogany, measuring 3/4″ x 3″ x 48″. Route a 1/2″ cove in one side and 1/2″ roundover on the other side as shown. After routing, cut one of the pieces into two 24″ sections for the side molding.

◆Cut the roundover side 3/4″ wide. Cut the cove side 1-1/4″ wide.

◆Set the roundover on top of the cove to form an ogee profile. Keeping the back even, glue and nail together with 1-1/4″ brads. Mark the area of the mitered corner; 17″-20″ from the back for the sides and 3″ from each end on the front molding piece. Do not put nails in this area. A spring clamp at each end will hold the moldings together while the glue dries. Sand the moldings prior to the next step.

◆Precision is essential! Letting the side pieces run long, cut the 45 degree miter for the front end and set aside. Cut one 45 degree miter on the long front piece. Mate the two miters together. Mark the back of the side molding for its straight cut. After making the straight cut, put the side molding in place, again using the front molding as a guide. Glue and nail into the side using 1-1/2″ brads. Do not glue to the top as it needs to be able to expand and contract throughout the seasons. Hold the front molding in place making sure the miter is tight and mark the far end miter. Glue the miters and nail. Finish the molding with the second side piece. Keeping the miter tight, mark for the straight cut, and install.

◆Completed trim.

◆Using 5/8″ brads and glue, attach the rear leg accents.

◆Miter one side of each of the front leg accents. This can be done on the table saw with a crosscut sled as they are too small to use a miter saw. Using 5/8″ brads and glue, attach the front leg accents.

Pocket Door Hardware

After trimming the doors to create a 1/8″ gap on the top, bottom, and hinge side, the hinge cups can be drilled per directions from the manufacturer. Two 3/4″ x 3″ x 20″ follower strips are required for the pocket door slides. Once the doors are hung, joint the edges where they meet in the center to leave a 1/16″ gap. Tilt the joiner's fence 5 degrees so the doors won't hit each other when closing one at a time.

◆Install a 3/4″ high x 1″ deep x 6″ long catch support centered on top rail. Use two 1 ½″ pocket screws to attach centering the support in the opening. Install double magnetic catches set 13/16 from the front edge of the case.

Drawers

Completed Case

The drawers were made using a Leigh D4 dovetail jig. This jig allows you to adjust the width of the pins and tails to mimic hand cut dovetails. With all drawer parts cut to size, make the dovetail joinery front and back as follows.

◆Mark 1/2″ and 1″ in from each side on the drawer sides.

◆Adjust the jig fingers to cover where the drawer bottom dado will be cut. Start with the fingers set in approximately 1/4″ from each edge.

◆Install a 7/16″ O.D. guide bushing and 1/2″ dovetail router bit in the router. An Infinity #18-135-8 12 degree bit is shown here.

◆Place a backer board behind the side to prevent chip out.

◆With the jig adjustment scales set at 5/8″, place the sliding dovetail bar in the fingers and make the first cut.

◆Remove the bar and rout the tails. Repeat the last step and rout the tails on each end for both side boards.

◆Flip over the jig finger assembly and place the drawer front in the jig. Use the drawer side as a stop, making sure it is below where the cuts will be.

◆Rout the pins on both ends. Install the drawer back and rout both ends.

◆After all of the dovetails are cut, install a dado cutter in the table saw set at 1/2″ wide x 1/4″ high. Cut the dado to hold the drawer bottom.

◆The dovetails should be snug, but not tight, and stay together without glue. The joints should be flush. After dry fitting all of the parts, apply glue to the tails, and assemble the drawer starting with a side and the drawer front.

◆Slide the bottom in place.

◆Tap the drawer back onto the drawer side.

◆Tap the remaining side into place. Use a wood scrap to put even pressure on the dovetails as they are tapped. Wipe off excess glue with a damp cloth. Measure from corner to corner to make sure the assembled drawer box is square. Set aside to dry and make the next drawer.

◆Completed drawer.

◆With the drawers in the case, mark for the hardware and drill.

Finishing

The same finishing recipe was used for the armoire as the bed. *See the finishing section at the end of the bed building instructions.*

Additional Plans

Side Table Build Sequence

1. Glue panel for top and shelf.
2. Shape legs.
3. Rout decorative edge on underside of top.
4. Build interior frames.
5. Build back and side frames.
6. Assemble back and side frames to legs (recess 1/8″ from leg).
7. Attach top interior frame.
8. Attach top to top interior frame (1″ overhang).
9. Attach bottom interior frame.
10. Attach shelf.
11. Install drawer guides.
12. Build drawer.

Side Table

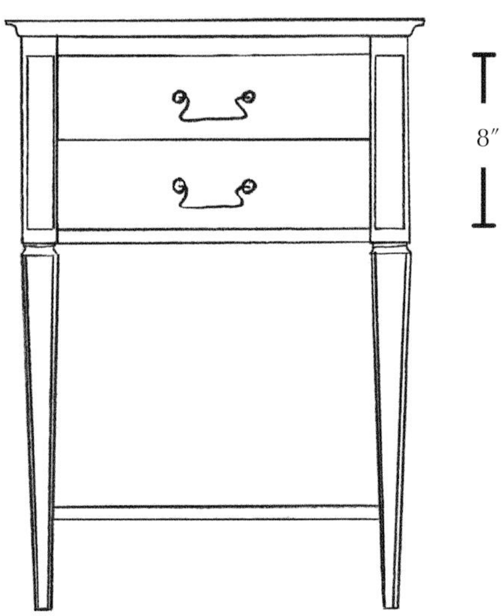

01 Front View

Side Table

02 Back & Side View

Side Table
Inner Frame View

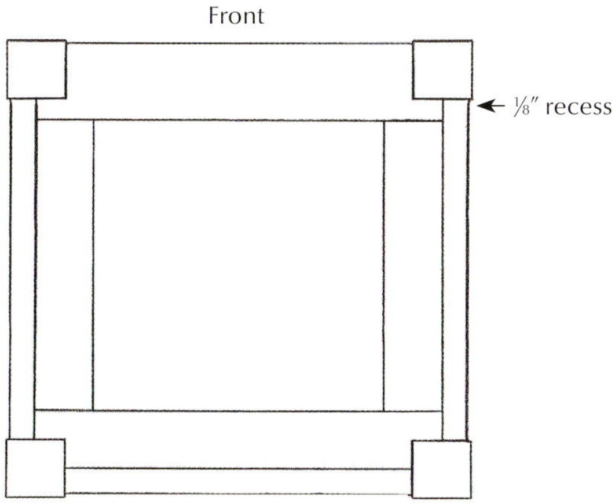

03

Legs

Cut 1 - dado 1/4″
wide x 3/32″ deep

04

Legs

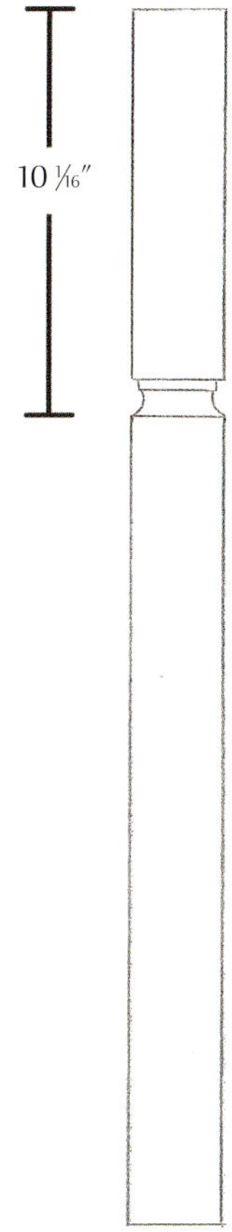

Cut 2 - use 1/2″ core box bit,
set 1/8″ high
Bit is MLCS #8717

05

45° jig for legs
1 - 15″ x 15″ made of 1/4″ plywood
1 - 3/4″ x 2″ x 15″ poplar

Cut "V" notch and attach to plywood
with 5/8″ brads

06

Legs

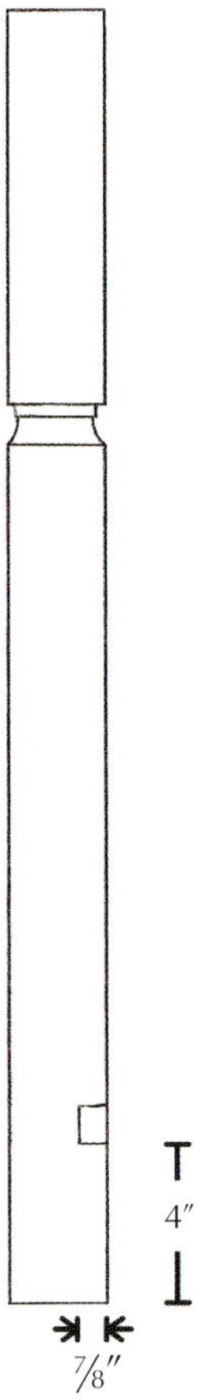

Cut 3: cut dado 3/4″ wide x 7/8″ deep in the inside corner of each leg using 45° jig

07

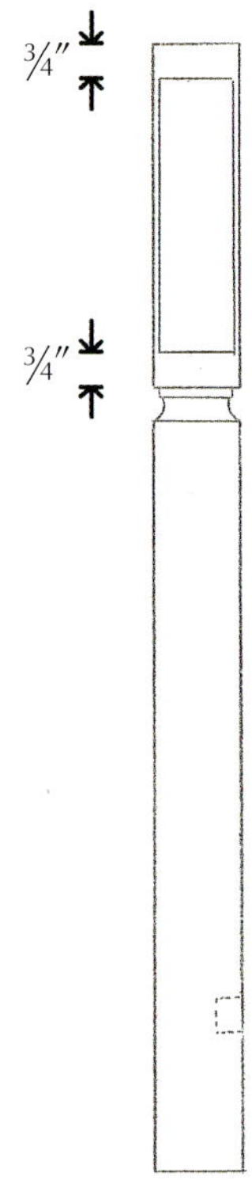

Cut 4: use template to rout recessed area (same procedure as armoire legs)
*front legs only

09

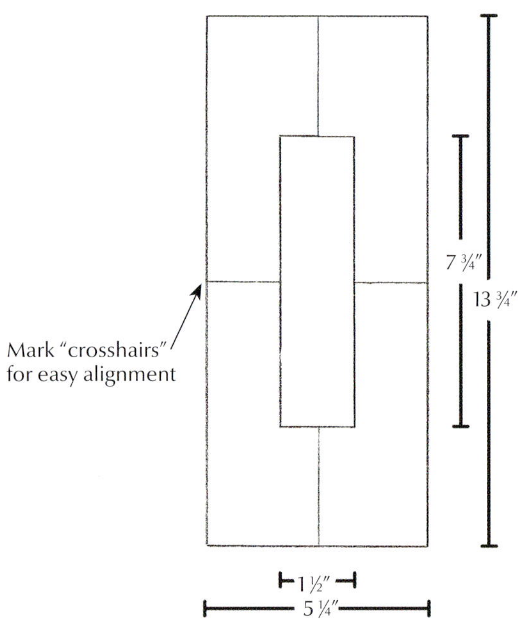

Leg Template for Recessed Area

08

Finishing leg cuts

Taper and bead legs as outlined with the armoire

10

Tenons

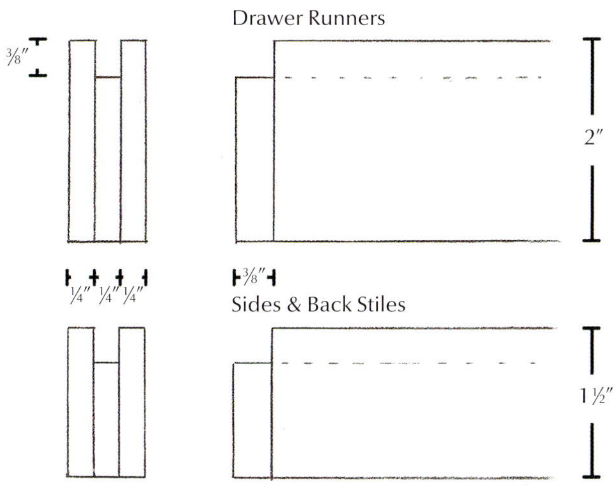

11

Top Detail (Router Profile - Ogee)

*Freud item # 38-106

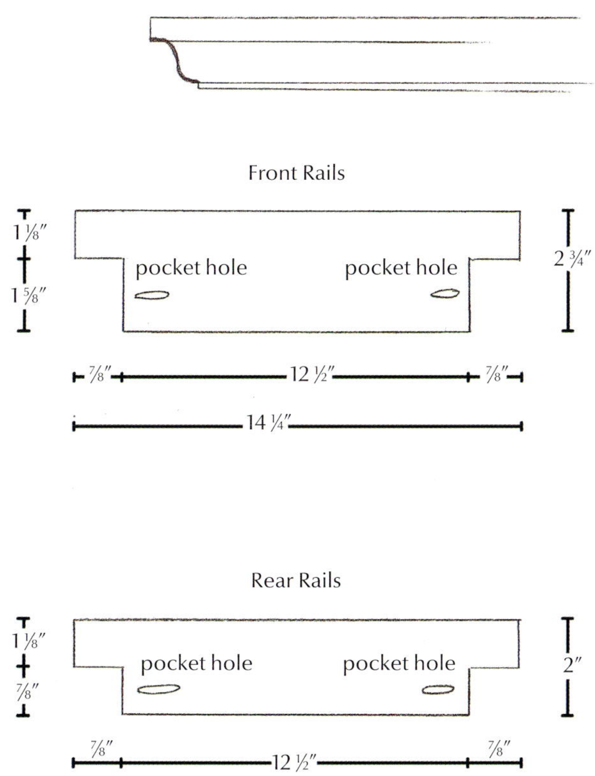

Side Table

12

Bottom Interior Frame (underside)

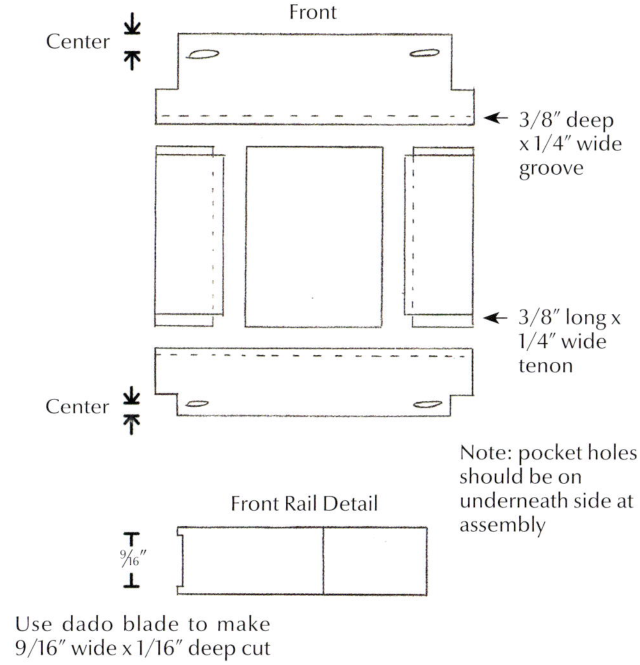

13

Sides and Back Assembly

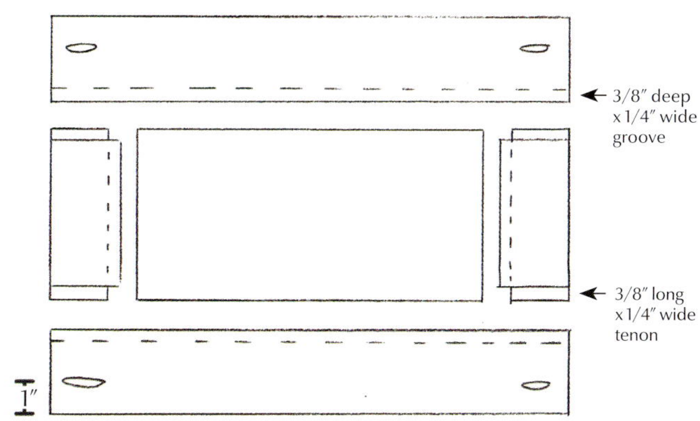

14

Top Interior Frame (top side)

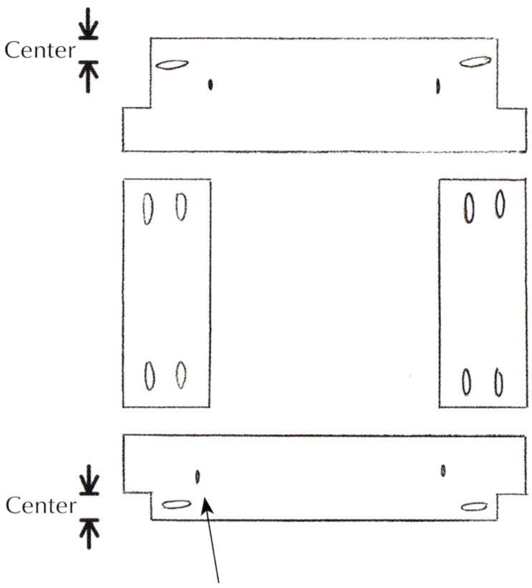

Drill (4) elongated 1/8″ diameter holes to attach top. This will allow for expansion & contraction of the top.

Note: pocket holes should be on top side at assembly

15

Bottom Interior Frame

Drawer Stops Placement

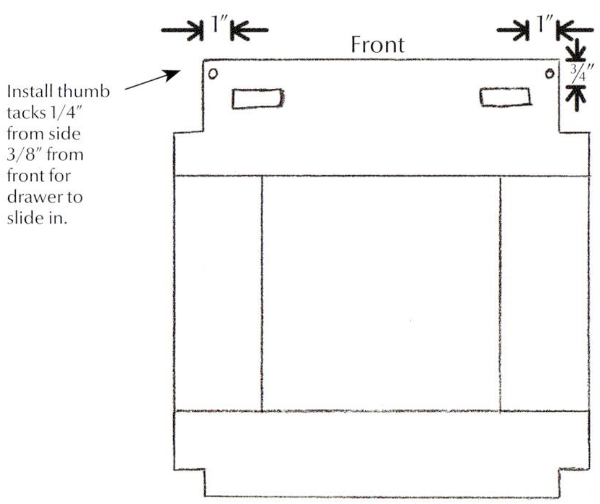

Attach drawer stops with 5/8″ brads and glue

Side View

16

Shelf

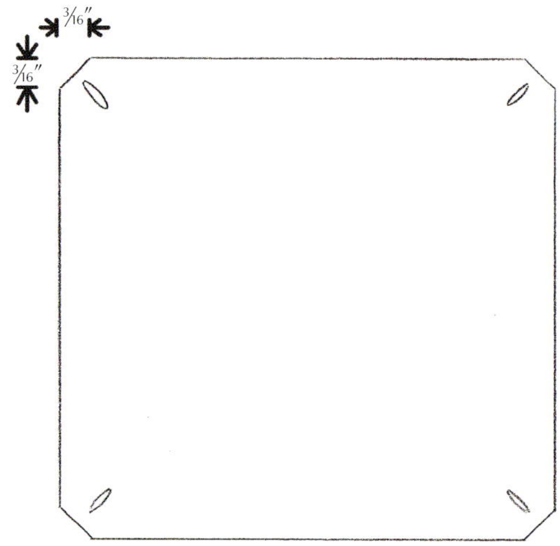

Cut 3/16″ from each corner at 45°

Drill pocket screws centered on angle cut

Pocket holes will be on the underneath side at assembly

17

Inner Frame View

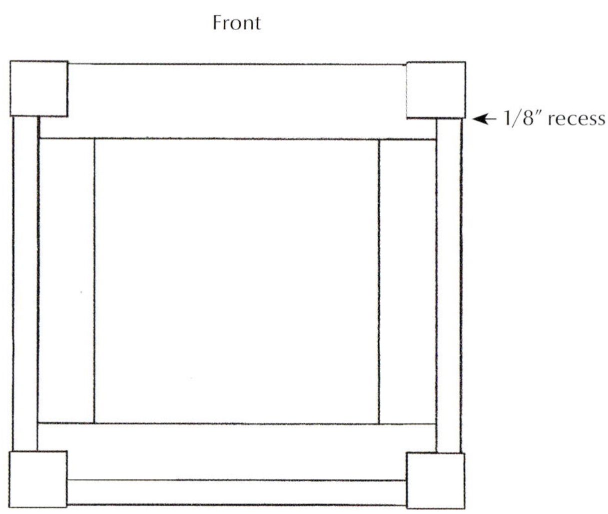

18

Suggested Dovetail Layout for Drawer

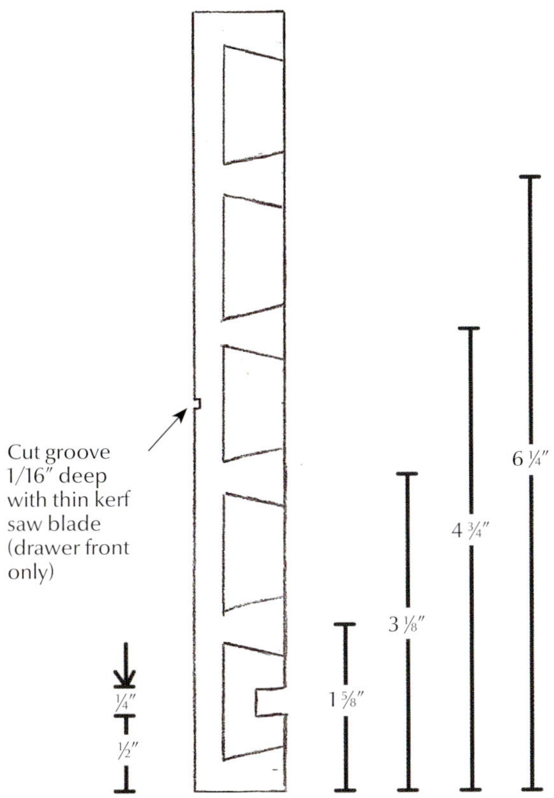

Cut groove in front, back and both sides 1/4″ wide x 1/4″ deep

19

Notches in Drawer Back

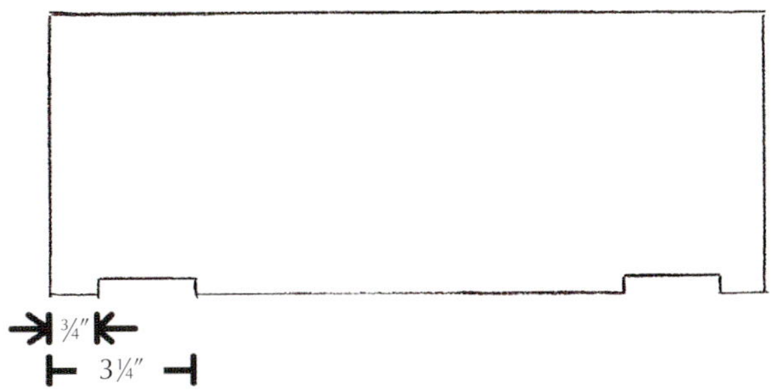

20

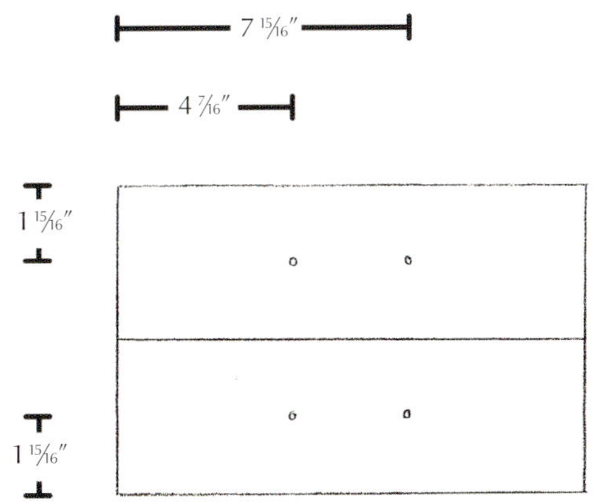

Drill 3/16″ diameter holes for hardware

Horton brasses # H-10FB, 3½″ light antique bail pull

21